Adoptable

ADOPTABLE

JESSICA GALLEGOS

Copyright © 2021 Jessica Gallegos

www.jessicagallegosauthor.com

ISBN 978-1-7370922-0-9 (paperback)
ISBN 978-1-7370922-1-6 (ebook)

Design: Heather McIntyre, Cover&Layout
Photography: House © DCA88; Hands © Ekkasit Rakrotchit

Printed in the United States of America

First Printing, 2021

This book is for all the children,
families, and providers working in and
with the systems of foster care.

INTRODUCTION

DYLAN IS A CHILD WITH special needs. He enters into foster care and takes everyone in his world on a journey full of ups and downs, twists and turns. It's a ride worth taking but rarely comfortable.

Dylan's story is based on actual experiences. All names, identifying features, and settings have been changed to protect the privacy and anonymity of all individuals in this book.

CHAPTER 1

SPIT HITS THE RIGHT SIDE of my face. A drop of it slides down my ear lobe. I take a deep breath, forcing the tightness building in my throat to relax. Another assault flies through the air and onto my right hand. I grip the steering wheel tighter. I almost gag at the faint smell of saliva and the cooling liquid on my cheek, but force myself not to react and to remain calm.

"Let's sing a song!" I say cheerfully. "Old MacDonald had a farm…"

"DOG!" comes Dylan's shouted reply from the back seat as I sing "E I E I O" and continue, "and on his farm he had a dog…" But the five-year-old behind me doesn't join in. Instead, I hear movement and grunting behind me. I glance in the rearview mirror. He's struggling. He's using one hand to open the front pocket of his jeans and the other to dig down deep inside. I stop singing and focus on the road ahead, grateful for this moment of distraction.

We've got another 40 minutes to go. I begin willing the stoplights to turn green. The sound of Dylan's grunt catches my attention again just as a puff of air hits my right cheek. A clattering sound directs my attention in front of me where a small, jagged rock has rolled to a stop between the windshield and dash. A second later, I feel a sharp pain and stinging on the back of my head. He has more rocks.

I shift my eyes to the rearview mirror. My heart races. Dylan is arching his back with one hand deep in his right pocket. He pulls out his hand, empty. My mood shifts from anxiety to anger. Pushing it down, I say as calmly as I can, "Dylan…" He's pulled off his shoes and one sock, shaking the contents out on his lap. We're coming to a red light, so I shift into a lower gear, slowing the car to a stop. The sound of sand and debris dancing on his lap is all I hear until Dylan sucks in his breath. I quickly turn around in my seat. Dylan has picked up a wood chip.

The playground we were on earlier had wood chips under the climbing equipment. I turn my head to see the light is still red, then turn back to Dylan, stretching out my hand to ask for the wood chip. As I reach out, Dylan jabs the wood chip forward and scrapes the inside of my right forearm. I jerk a bit at the pain and my left foot slips off the clutch. The car lurches forward and the engine dies.

This distracts Dylan for an instant. "Uht's wong, Skiska? Car boken?"

"Nope. The car is fine," I say as I turn back around in my seat and start the car again. Dylan had trouble with pronunciation and "Skiska" was how he pronounced my name. The light turns green and we move forward. "Dylan, give me the wood chip." I reach my hand back toward him, keeping my eyes on the road; praying he doesn't attack me with it again. I look in the rearview again and he's looking out the window, gnawing on the wood chip.

This drive with Dylan was not unusual. He always exhibited these types of behaviors. Especially in the car. And especially on the way to or on the way back from a family visit with his biological mother and siblings. Anxiety and fear, a general feeling of being unsafe, caused Dylan to act out in a variety of behaviors. The behaviors ranged from mild to extreme, often within a few minutes.

I glance at my watch. About 30 minutes to go until we are at his foster home in a suburb of Phoenix, and I'm free. In the rearview mirror I can see Dylan continuing to gnaw on the wood chip. Saliva is drooling out of his mouth and dripping onto his shirt. Another glance at my watch. Twenty-five minutes to go. The loud, clear sound of road noise cuts into my thoughts. *Dang it!* I forgot to engage the child locks. Dylan has opened the car door and pulled it shut again. "Leave the door closed, Dylan." He opens it again and spits out the little bits of wood from his mouth. The pounding in my chest is so strong it almost hurts. A vision of Dylan falling out of the car onto the road and into traffic flashes before my eyes. I begin to slow down and look for a place to pull over. *He's still buckled*, I try to reassure myself.

He pulls the door shut again and shouts "Wass dat?" while pointing to a billboard.

"It says, *Need new tires?*" My voice is shaking a little.

"Wass dat say?" he says, pointing to another sign.

I read the words out loud and take a deep breath. This is a common activity for us. He points to billboards and signs and asks what they say. I tell him and he continues. It can go on for an entire car ride or for a few minutes. I'm hoping this time it will continue until we get to his house.

We had had a 90-minute drive to Globe, a city East of Phoenix, then a two-hour visit with his family, and now another 90-minute drive back after a stop at McDonald's. I always took Dylan to McDonald's when I took him anywhere. Eventually, it became a bargaining chip, and eventually, I became angry at myself for letting it get to that point. Dylan and cars didn't mix well, because he became quite anxious. His therapist had shared that he likely felt out of control and unsafe in a car. She said the longer he spent in a car the more extreme his behaviors would be, and that if we could, we should keep his car rides to a minimum.

"Hep me, hep me!" Dylan began shouting. He had wiggled down into the seat so that the seatbelt was up to his armpits and he was kicking. His entire torso was on the seat, his head and arms sticking out above the seatbelt, his legs and hips totally off the seat. He kept kicking. "HEEEP!" he screeched, his voice becoming raspy. The more he kicked and writhed, the redder his face got. I reached back with my right hand and did my best to help him, while staying on the road. We weren't in a space that was safe to pull over and he wasn't being strangled, as far as I could see. He was just stuck and probably uncomfortable.

He continued his struggle and a couple of miles later I pulled over onto the shoulder of the highway. I turned off the car and got out. The road was pretty quiet, with few cars passing us. I slowly walked around the back, breathing deeply, and reached his door on the other side. I opened it and helped him get out of the seat belt. He started to wriggle out of the car. I held him in place and gently but firmly put him back in his seat. When I reached over to buckle him he grabbed my head and neck. I braced for a bite but he gave me a big sloppy kiss on my ear.

"I love you, Skiska."

"I love you too, Dylan."

"We almosss home?"

"Yes, we are very close to home now." I engaged the child lock before shutting the door, got back in the car, back on the road. The lead foot I had inherited from my great-grandmother kicked in, and we cut five minutes off our normal travel time.

CHAPTER 2

I WAS EXHAUSTED AS I pulled up to the two-story, mocha-colored, stucco home with cheerful flowers and shrubs framing the concrete walk. The majority of homes in Phoenix and surrounding cities are stucco, styled after Mediterranean designs. "Dylan, we're home."

"Mom!" he called out, fumbling with the buckle a little. I open his door and in a flash he was on the sidewalk, quickly stumbling toward the house. "Ah!" Down he went, hands and knees on the sidewalk.

"Oh! Dylan, are you okay?" I crouched to help him up and check out his knees and palms of his hands. A few pale scratch lines on his palms were all I could see before he wriggled away from me, continuing his path.

His foster mom stepped out, bent down and hugged him. "Hey, you two," Jane greeted us. When she saw me, she knew what kind of trip we had likely had. She smiled and took him inside. I turned back to the car and grabbed Dylan's backpack, shoes, one sock, and my purse. I did a second sweep, looking for the second sock but couldn't locate it, hoping it was still on him somewhere. I walked up to the house and let myself in the front door. Jane was getting Dylan cleaned up in the hall bathroom.

"Jessica, how was your day?" she said with kindness and a knowing tone. I smiled at her and shared how Dylan's day had been, what Dylan's teacher had told me when I picked him up from school, how our trip to and from the visit was, and how the actual visit was. I gave the facts, keeping it positive. By this time Dylan was crawling up the stairs to see his foster brothers and sister. He was five years old but hadn't mastered walking up or down stairs yet. Jane followed him and brought all the kids downstairs to play in the living room while we finished our talk. We sat on the couch and I pulled out a form to document the home visit.

While we talked, I shared details of the visit. The children were nearby so I left out some details and used a positive tone. The details of Dylan's behaviors both at the visit and in the car would be shared out of earshot of Dylan and the other children.

Typically, a foster home receives one home visit each month for the purpose of monitoring. Licensing, certification renewals, updated guidelines, and anything pertaining to the foster placement is discussed. Doctor visits, school or day programs, home life, and sleeping and eating patterns are all documented, as well as how the foster family is doing. The foster placement's case is also discussed along with upcoming visits, court dates, therapies, and Foster Care Review Board meetings (FCRB).

I quickly went into more detail on the things we had discussed while Dylan was getting cleaned up earlier. A scream erupted from the floor in front of us. Jane's 4-year-old daughter had a book in both her hands and Dylan had the same book in his hands, as well as his mouth.

"I had it first!" she cried. Jane was on the floor instantly, her hand circled around Dylan's torso just as he lunged for his foster sister. He immediately began spitting and laughing. I watched a moment, allowing Jane to take control of the situation. I also made a mental note of the incident so I could document it in my observations along with the day's earlier events. These notes would be submitted to Dylan's case manager and his therapist.

Jane got the kids settled down. Dylan followed Jane to the couch and attempted to climb onto her lap. She helped him up and he leaned against her, playing with her hands. It was getting late, so we clarified a few upcoming dates for court and therapy as well as the next two visits with the biological mom and wrapped up the visit.

I got up as Dylan was attempting to put Jane's fingers in his mouth. She was fumbling with his hands and hers and giving him the cues for what was coming next, bath and bed. I grabbed my notes, folder, and purse and headed toward the door. Jane stood Dylan on the ground and held his hand as she walked me out. She called over her shoulder to the other children to head upstairs and get ready for bed. There was a little protest, and then the rumbling sound of feet climbing the stairs.

Jane thanked me for all that I did that day. I smiled in return and said, "Thank YOU, for all that you do every day." The words weren't enough and felt empty in a way. I bent down to Dylan and told him I'd see him next week. As I walked to my car, I could hear the sound of Dylan's voice hollering, "Hungry!"

As I started my car my own stomach grumbled. In response I felt my hands begin to shake as I turned the steering wheel, guiding the car out of the neighborhood. I mentally ran down the list of fast-food restaurants, eliminating any without a drive-through. It was fully dark now and I did not want to get out of my car again until I reached home. There was a Taco Bell on the way that would satisfy my hunger and need for a drive-through. That settled, my mind focused back on Jane, Dylan, and the following workday.

CHAPTER 3

I MOVED TO TEMPE, A suburb of Phoenix, Arizona, the last week of 2004. I was moving in with my boyfriend, the man who would later become my husband. I had been living in the Tucson area, about two hours south of Phoenix, since 1992. This move would be the first time I moved away from the area of my immediate family. It was scary and exciting. I was leaving a stable job with no new one in sight and was taking a chance on love. I didn't know which was riskier.

The first days of 2005, I applied at a few companies I felt would be a good fit for me and put to good use my ten years of experience working with children. I was also going to university to finish my Bachelor's degree in Sociology. Because I was taking distance and online classes mostly, my schedule was very flexible. This was good because I needed a full-time position. By Wednesday, January 5, I had three interviews lined up. The first, on Thursday the 6th, was with an agency providing education and social services to families of children with developmental disabilities.

The agency, Child Connections, was very small, very warm, and very welcoming. At the interview, I felt as if I had met longtime friends. I was impressed with owners, Bob and Faith, and the family-centered, yet professional, atmosphere they had created. The interview lasted about two hours. We had been so absorbed in the conversation that time got away from us. When Faith noticed the time, her eyes widened and she said, "Oh geez, we'd better let you get out of here before traffic gets too bad." I laughed, thanked them, and said I didn't think it would be too bad. Faith made a comment about Phoenix traffic and a few minutes later as I was merging onto the I-17 I saw exactly what she was talking about. Ten minutes later I was only a mile away from the office, attempting to merge onto the freeway, when my cellphone rang.

It was Bob. My heart picked up a beat. "Faith and I were talking, and I told her we couldn't let you interview with anyone else and miss our chance. We'd like to offer you the position." I swallowed a squeal and as calmly as I could, accepted the job, and thanked him with probably a little too much gusto. Bob asked if I could start on Monday, to which I replied yes, and asked what time.

When I started with Child Connections my position was as a Developmental Special Instructor, or DSI. Our agency was contracted with the State of Arizona to provide Early Intervention services to children from birth to age three. I would visit families in their homes and coach, teach, and support them in meeting the needs of their child with special needs. The children were all under the age of three. Some had been diagnosed with a developmental disability and some were delayed enough in their development that they needed support to meet typical milestones. Sometimes I attended doctor's appointments, therapy visits, childcare centers, and court hearings, or attended visitations for the children who were in foster care. The position required me to be part teacher and part social worker. Most visits were no more than information-sharing; walking a new mom through the lists of therapists and developmental pediatricians and what those visits might look like for her and her child. Some visits were very hands-on, on the ground, interacting and playing with a child while encouraging the parent to get down on the floor with us and engage as much as possible to get the child to engage. Often, in the beginning of working with a new family, parts of visits were spent observing the child and family in their daily environment. Observation was one of my favorite tools. It gave me the information necessary to help a family develop a plan of action, action to give their child the best possible start in life. Occasionally I would be assigned to a family and soon realize they were doing everything right and my role was unnecessary. Those cases were some of the most difficult. The parents would be such high achievers that they were convinced there was more they could be doing or doing differently to help their child. The only thing they didn't have control over was time, which made some parents impatient. Time, consistency, and patience are not taught much in our "instant gratification" society.

One mom I worked with was certain she wasn't doing enough. Her husband traveled three weeks a month and it was up to her to manage everything at home. She took her two-year-old son to speech and occupational therapy twice a week; she had signed him up for a music therapy class; she had purchased so many children's books and learning toys that their living room and child's bedroom were explosions of bright colors and electronic sounds. Any suggestion a professional or book suggested, this mom put it into action. Each week I struggled to meet the mother's expectations. I got so caught up in her desire for action, doing more, that I lost sight of the basics of early-childhood development. Children learn in the context of relationship and with repetition. It took another couple of months of coaching to help the mother understand that her child didn't need "more", he needed her. She had been so focused on giving resources to him that she had taken herself out of the equation. Therapies and toys are excellent, but the missing ingredient is often the parent.

I convinced her to remove half of the toys, store them for later, and set up a schedule for her and her son to play. During play, she was to be key ingredient. She would use techniques she learned from therapies with her son. She would incorporate lots of snuggle-time in between playtimes. When she read books to her son, she would let him lead. If they read the same page 12 times, that was okay. Her son's language and motor skills continued a slow, steady progress. His social-emotional skills progressed so rapidly it was astounding.

The mother was elated, but soon realized she was feeling overwhelmed. I asked if she had someone in her family or friend group whom she trusted and that her son felt comfortable with. Her mother-in-law was that person. She was just as committed to the child's well-being and willing to help out. I then worked with the grandmother, coaching her and bringing her up to speed in a way that supported the mother and child, but didn't take over the mother's role. It was an excellent addition to the child's intervention plan.

Another family I worked with was a completely different situation. When I met the teenage mother of an 18-month-old, it was like pulling teeth to get the young mother to even speak to me. She was so unsure of her world and her child. The first month working with her was spent mostly on building a relationship with mom and modeling how to interact with the child who was not yet talking or walking. I learned that the mother thought a quiet baby was a good baby. With some education and instruction, she soon learned how to interact with her child and be her child's first teacher. A few months of visits and the mother was beginning to come up with ideas of activities on her own. She had very little in terms of toys but was able to see how everyday items like plastic food containers were just as interesting to her child. Her biggest struggle was that she was a child herself and found it difficult to balance her own needs with the needs of her child. Her child's development progressed consistently, but very slowly.

I absolutely loved my job. I felt useful, helpful, and part of a team, and soon my role blossomed to include more leadership and responsibilities. I was helping at staff meetings, asking to attend further training, helping train new staff, and I started an agency newsletter for staff and the families we served. About six months in, Bob and Faith had noticed my enjoyment in training others and asked me to become a certified Red Cross CPR/First Aid Instructor. They said it would help them to have a trainer available for employees as well as for our Developmental Home Foster Care providers. I jumped at the opportunity and was ready for more.

Child Connections had two programs, the Early Intervention Services program and the Developmental Home Foster Care program. I didn't know much about the latter program other than the two employees, so I set up a time with Elizabeth, who ran that program, to tell me more about it. I wanted to know more about what foster-care providers did so I could understand what situations they might be in regularly, and also so I could incorporate articles and information in the agency newsletter that would be useful for everyone involved with the agency.

Several months later Faith approached me and asked if I would be interested in applying for the Developmental Home Program as a licensing specialist. Feeling needed and appreciated is like a drug to me, so I jumped at the chance to interview for the position. Since speaking with Elizabeth about the Developmental Home Program months earlier, I had become even more interested in the work, reading articles about foster care in Arizona and becoming familiar with the Arizona Department of Economic Security and Division of Developmental Disabilities rules and regulations.

I could not have foreseen how much this new role would give me, nor how much it would take from me.

CHAPTER 4

OFTEN WHEN A CHILD IS in need of a foster home the placement occurs quickly. Before joining the Maxwell home, Dylan had been removed from his mother's care to the care of his maternal grandmother. Within a week it was evident his grandmother was not capable of safely meeting his very extensive needs. She asked for him to be removed and began packing his clothes.

The calls requesting for foster placement, come in on an almost emergency basis. This is the case for most foster-care placements. In Dylan's case: a four-year-old boy needed placement within 24 hours. Child Protective Services was requesting a foster home that was either skilled in working with children with higher needs or for a Developmental Foster Home. A Developmental Foster Home is one in which the providers (foster parents) have gone through specialized training to provide care for a child or an adult with developmental disabilities. The Division of Developmental Disabilities licenses these specialized foster homes.

The Maxwells were ready, available, and as equipped as they could be. They prepared a second bed in their youngest son's bedroom for Dylan.

Jane and Phillip Maxwell had three children, two boys, and a girl in the middle. Phillip worked outside the home in the technology field, while Jane focused on the home and children. The oldest child, Tyler, was in second grade, Cassie was in preschool, and Jonathan, 2, was home with mom. As dedicated Christians, they felt called to serve their community through fostering.

Elizabeth, the family's licensing specialist at that time, called the Maxwells, gave them the details provided (there are never enough details), and they agreed to take the placement. Elizabeth contacted the Case Manager, David, and formally accepted the placement. David and a case aide picked up Dylan and began the three-hour drive to Phoenix from Safford, Arizona. The Maxwell family lived in a suburb of Phoenix, in a quiet neighborhood full of families and young professionals. The children attended school and preschool just two miles from home.

When David and the case aide arrived with Dylan, it was dark outside. They helped Dylan out of the car and up to the house. Elizabeth had arrived about an hour before to visit with the family and help prepare them for their first foster child. The doorbell rang and as Phillip opened the door, a high-pitched growling sound filled the front room. He glanced down and saw a very small, blond boy with brilliant blue eyes, baring his teeth, chin gleaming with saliva. Phillip stepped aside, and welcomed David, Dylan, and the aide into the home. They sped through introductions as Dylan thrashed and continually attempted to bite the case aide who had a firm hold on him.

Elizabeth and the family stared, somewhat in shock at the small child in front of them, smaller than a four-year-old should be. Jane quickly knelt down and made eye contact with Dylan. "Hi. I'm Jane. Are you hungry?" Dylan paused a moment. Jane looked at the case aide and said, "I'll take him." She took him under the arms, picked him up, and carried him into the kitchen. Everyone else followed. Dylan began to thrash his body as he looked around. Jane spoke to Phillip and suggested he and the case aide take the other children into the living room, leaving just three adults with Dylan in the kitchen. Dylan immediately calmed to half the intensity. Jane opened a pudding cup and handed Dylan a spoon. He threw the spoon across the table and pushed the cup into his face. Pudding squished out the sides of the cup and Dylan smeared the pudding with his hand and began sucking on his fingers. Jane retrieved the spoon and scooped some pudding from the mostly empty cup. She put it up to Dylan and he bit down on the spoon before sucking the pudding off it. They continued this until the pudding was gone. Dylan wiped his pudding covered hands on the table as Jane got up and ran a paper towel under the faucet. She cleaned him up and took him by the hand to the living room, announcing it was bedtime.

The Maxwell children were already in their pajamas. The children and family marched upstairs. David, Elizabeth, and the case aide waited downstairs. They could hear the Maxwells putting the children down to bed. David turned to the case aide and stated that after the kids were down, she should go up to Dylan's room to keep an eye on him while he met with the Maxwells and Elizabeth. She agreed and headed upstairs. There was some quiet discussion and the Maxwells came down.

David gave a brief history of Dylan's experience in foster care and followed with specifics about his behaviors observed so far. The Maxwells and Elizabeth asked many questions and David answered them as honestly and thoroughly as possible. They discussed school, therapies, and doctor's visits that would need to be scheduled and how to go about that. David, as a representative of the State, was Dylan's legal guardian. He provided the necessary paperwork they would need in order to be able to register Dylan for preschool, take him to the doctor, or for any other needs that might arise.

The case aide came downstairs and let everyone know that Dylan was asleep. The group met for a few more minutes. David and the case aide said good-bye and began their long drive home. Elizabeth stayed just a few minutes more, making sure the Maxwells felt comfortable. They said they did and would call her in the morning with an update.

CHAPTER 5

A FEW HOURS AFTER THE Maxwells had gone to bed, they woke to the sound of crying from their youngest son. Jane got up and went in to check on Jonathan and Dylan. Dylan was stumbling back and forth from his bed to Jonathan's bed. Each time he reached Jonathan, he would grab Jonathan's legs and squeeze.

Jane went to Dylan and picked him up. He began wriggling his body and kicking her. She hugged him and began gently bouncing and turning back and forth as she would an infant. He calmed after almost two minutes. She put him back in bed and rubbed his back until he went to sleep. Jonathan had stopped crying but was wide awake. Jane went to him, picked him up and took him to sleep with her and Phillip.

Another hour later, she was back in the bedroom with Dylan, repeating her earlier motions and finally getting him back to sleep. He didn't get up again until the sun rose. Jane and Phillip were startled awake by a loud crash. Phillip got up this time and found Dylan in the middle of the room with a bin of large plastic blocks dumped out and scattered all around. Phillip ducked as Dylan threw a block at him, laughing. By this time everyone was awake and they began the morning routine, with breakfast and getting ready for school. Phillip handled Tyler, Cassie, and Jonathan while Jane took care of Dylan.

On the phone later that morning, Jane described the previous night and that morning in detail to Elizabeth and said she felt she would need at least two more hands to deal with Dylan. They both laughed. Jane said she'd get all Dylan's appointments set up that day and let Elizabeth know if she needed something. Before hanging up, Jane commented that Dylan must not have heard about the "honeymoon period," with the behaviors she had already seen.

The honeymoon period is a term often used to describe the period of time after a child is placed into a foster home. The child and foster family are often on their best behavior and everything seems to go smoothly. This period can last anywhere from a few days to a few months. At the end of the honeymoon period the foster child may begin exhibiting behaviors in response to their emotional state and the environment around them, and may act out, sometimes in violent ways. The honeymoon period doesn't always occur. A more accurate way to describe this period of time is by calling it a transitional period. Some foster children and foster families transition well, some don't, and sometimes it just depends on the environment. Dylan did not do well with transitions.

Two weeks later, Elizabeth was filing the fifth incident documentation into Dylan's file and preparing to send a copy to David, the case manager. Dylan's file was full of documentation. Reading through it felt like a ride on a roller coaster. A roller coaster that went fast and slow but never stopped.

A change to one's environment creates a ripple. Like a rock dropped into a body of water. The ripple begins at the point of contact and travels outward. When the contact is significant enough, the ripple will travel out to the edge of the body of water and bounce back toward the starting place. For individuals with heightened senses, whether from traumatic experiences, chronic stress, or coming into this world exquisitely sensitive, any change to the environment becomes an experience. An experience in slow motion. Every moment is new, often overwhelming, and is a feeling that has to be dealt with.

Routine and consistency are the heroes for those with special needs. They are like a soft, warm blanket that offer protection from the transitions of the world.

CHAPTER 6

THE FOLLOWING MORNING, AS THE sun began to wake up the valley, Elizabeth heard from Jane Maxwell. She heard from her again the next morning and the next, and almost daily the following two weeks.

Jane had questions. Dylan was her first foster child. How did she go about finding the right doctor and dentist? Would they need to find a special sitter when Jane and Phillip wanted a date night?

She wanted advice and reassurance. Many mornings Jane would wake to find clothes and toys strewn about, pieces of ripped paper in odd places, and wet spots. What were those wet spots? She found them on the carpet, on bedding, on clothing, on the curtains. What should she say when Dylan mentioned his mom? How should she discipline him when he acted out?

During the orientation and training process to become foster parents, these topics and many more were discussed, but it is difficult to remember everything when the first placement comes into your home. Parenting your own children is one thing, parenting someone else's child can be tricky.

Elizabeth listened to the uncertainty and anxiety in Jane's questions. She had concerns that Dylan might be too much for this young family and turn them off of foster care. Foster care is a temporary situation and agencies, like Child Connections, relied on families to continue fostering. The alternative to a foster home was a group home, and children almost always fare better in a stable family home environment. Elizabeth didn't voice her concerns but she did make extra phone calls to check in and stayed longer than usual at the home for monitoring visits to give some extra support. She also attended some doctor and therapy appointments at Jane's request. This turned out to be an on-going practice, as it supported Dylan's best interests.

Jane also had incident reports to make. Bumps, bruises, biting, and scratches were almost a daily occurrence. Sometimes Dylan was the one with the injuries. He had very poor balance and body control. He fell a lot, tripping on the sidewalk and bumping into things. He was also the cause of many injuries. Scratching and biting were common in the beginning.

More frequent than the injuries, but less reported, were the toileting difficulties. Dylan came into care wearing pull-ups. He wasn't potty trained yet but did have an interest in using the toilet. This is not unusual, especially for children with special needs. However, it wasn't just that Dylan wasn't potty trained, or that he wanted to use the toilet. Dylan also acted out at times by urinating on things, and by fecal smearing. A child's behavior is a way of expressing needs. Dylan had a lot of needs.

Dylan's case manager, David, was also in regular contact with both Elizabeth and Jane. He was free with Dylan's information as it pertained to his care, sharing anything that might be helpful, or giving insight into Dylan's needs and history. He was also very responsive to any calls Elizabeth or Jane made to him.

Consistency was a strength of Jane's, and it is a trait foster care agencies and those working at the Department of Economic Security look for in foster care providers. When a child can fit into a home that is consistent and loving, it gives that child a stronger chance at "settling in" in a shorter amount of time, which supports the child's overall emotional needs and success. Consistency in the daily routine, in the language the family uses, in the activities the family engages in, all set a predictable stage for a child to grasp and begin to understand their world.

For Dylan, a child with significant special needs, consistency and routine became the family's lifeline.

Dylan attached to Jane quickly and began calling her mom the first week. It is common for children to call foster parents "mom" and "dad" because the other children in the home call them that. This can be difficult for the biological family to understand.

He hugged Jane any chance he could get and held on tight. He also hugged his foster siblings and foster father. He attempted slobbery kisses to anyone he got close enough to. Dylan laughed easily and hollered "Hi!" any time someone entered a room. He was so excited for almost every new experience, especially if he was with Jane.

One day not long after Dylan joined the Maxwells, Jane was taking the children to Walmart to do some shopping for the household and to get Dylan some new clothes. She got them all buckled in the minivan and set out. About five minutes away from home Dylan unbuckled himself and had slid open the van door. As quickly as she could without slamming on the brakes, Jane stopped the van on the side of the road. Luckily, they were still in a residential area and were not traveling very fast. As soon as the van stopped Dylan hopped out, fell on the ground and began to crawl away from the van. Jane ran around to where Dylan was making a slow escape and picked him up. She hugged him first, trying to calm her pounding heart, then began the talk that she would endlessly repeat for the next four years. "We keep the seatbelts buckled in the car. You never get out of your seat until I say it's okay. Never open the door. You could get hurt …."

The other children's voices began to filter in as the beating of her heart slowed. "Mom! Is he okay? He just jumped out!" Dylan was growling and kicking his feet against Jane and trying to wriggle out of her grasp.

Jane got Dylan back in the van, buckled him in, and engaged the child safety locks. The rest of the drive she was hyper alert and every minute or two reminded all the children to keep their seatbelts buckled. When they arrived at the store Jane was ready for anything, but the rest of the trip was mostly uneventful except for constantly redirecting Dylan and telling him to take merchandise out of his mouth every few minutes.

Dylan regularly unbuckled his seatbelt. The Maxwells asked everyone associated with Dylan's care what they could do about it. His Case Manager and guardian, David, was in the process of getting a vehicle safety restraint approved through the court. In the meantime, the family would have to do its best.

CHAPTER 7

THERE WERE MANY STORIES ABOUT Dylan's biological family and their history. Like a game of *Telephone*, the more the stories were shared the more they varied. It was almost impossible to get a clear picture or history. Often whomever was sharing information was also adding their thoughts and suppositions. Each social worker's or support person's experience with the biological family was shared through the lens of that person. They put their own feelings and biases into the equation.

Dylan originally lived with his mother, Sabrina, and three siblings. He had an older brother and sister, and one younger sister. Dylan and his two older siblings shared a father who was not in the children's lives. The youngest sibling's father lived with the family most of the time. He worked in construction, and some jobs took him to nearby towns for several days. Sabrina worked short periods of time while the children were in school and day care. Dylan never lasted long in day care, due to his behaviors.

Sabrina's mother, Cathy, once told a caseworker from Child Protective Services (CPS) that Sabrina was the laziest mother she'd ever seen. A mother who couldn't feed her kids, let them run all over the place, and let her boyfriend beat them. To another caseworker Cathy seemed supportive and sympathetic, saying that Sabrina tried very hard to provide for her children and was doing her best. Cathy explained that the kids were bad and that was the reason CPS had been called. There had been several CPS reports over the years.

Sabrina's own childhood may provide some insight. She was an only child. Her father left the home when Sabrina was in middle school. She had contact with him, but irregularly, because he was a truck driver. Her mother, Cathy, relied on her ex-husband's child support to provide for the majority of their expenses. She worked part-time jobs sporadically. When she wasn't working, she was keeping the modest house they lived in. Cathy was very strict in her rules for life. She believed a home should be clean. A person should not want more than they are given. One should not trust others easily. When Sabrina was growing up, Cathy was like a drill sergeant. If Sabrina left a glass on the coffee table, she would be berated and sent to her room.

In stark contrast as an adult, Sabrina took little care of her home. She let the children eat all over the house, which was dirty and cluttered. Surfaces were often sticky with peanut butter and jelly. The home felt stuffy and had a slight sour smell to it. The three-bedroom house was small. Built in the 1980's, it was efficient and stable, though no updates had improved the home in 20 years. Dylan and his brother shared one room, his two sisters another, and Sabrina and her boyfriend, her youngest child's father, shared what might be called a master bedroom though not much distinguished it apart from the other two rooms. The home had one bathroom. Mildew, mold, and all manner of smells kept one from staying in the home too long.

When Dylan was first removed by Child Protective Services, it wasn't the first time the family had a report of abuse or neglect. Reports from neighbors, teachers, and an extended family member were all recorded. Sabrina was interviewed, a general assessment was completed, and action steps were directed to her. She was warned each time that if she didn't "clean up her act" the children would be removed. It wasn't until after the third or fourth report that all the children were removed and placed in the care of their grandmother, Cathy. This was considered a temporary arrangement. Services would be put in place for Sabrina and a court date was set to evaluate the case and determine next steps.

It was soon apparent that Cathy's home was not a long-term option. The environment the grandmother provided was less neglectful and less abusive, but soon determined unsafe for all the children. Cathy expected the children to follow directions and when they didn't, or couldn't, she yelled, threatened, and punished the children. Dylan's behaviors escalated. After only four days Cathy called the Child Protective Services Case Manager and said she didn't want the kids any longer and that she couldn't handle Dylan. She characterized him as an animal. Child Protective Services removed Dylan from Cathy's care and convinced her to keep her other three grandchildren a bit longer until a more suitable foster home could be located.

Dylan went into foster care. A beautiful little boy with bright eyes and a quick smile, Dylan was welcomed with open arms to his first foster home. A week later, he was welcomed with open arms to his second foster home. Two days later, the CPS Case Manager contacted the Division of Developmental Disabilities and began the process to transfer Dylan's case. It was clear that his behaviors indicated something more was going on. He showed delays in the areas of motor skills, speech, cognitive, and social-emotional development. His siblings showed no developmental delays.

Neither foster home was equipped to care for a child with such significant behaviors. During meals Dylan would shovel food into his mouth, barely chew it, and then swallow, causing him to gag and often regurgitate the food. He could continue this through an entire meal. Drinks were spilled at almost every meal and a sippy cup was used. The sippy cup also helped him slow down drinking. Food was cut up into small bites and each meal was a new experience, waiting to see what would stay down, what would come up, and what might end up on the floor or on someone else.

Dylan wasn't potty-trained yet and diapering him was extremely difficult. He attempted to scratch and bite whoever was changing him. Changing him on the floor was the safest place, as he often thrashed his body about.

His behaviors swung from extremely unpleasant and unsafe to extremely adorable. He smiled most of the time, hugged everyone, and laughed infectiously.

One of the services provided by the Division of Developmental Disabilities in Arizona is Licensed Developmental Foster Homes. Foster families with this special license attend specialized training designed to better meet the needs of a child with special developmental needs.

CHAPTER 8

THE FIRST TIME I MET Dylan, he had been brought to our office for a court-ordered visitation with his biological mother. I was still working as a Developmental Special Instructor for our Early Intervention program and was in the office for a few minutes to drop off some paperwork and pick up some supplies. I was sitting at one of the community computers emailing, when the front door opened. I heard Elizabeth's voice and the breathing, no, panting of a small child. Clumping, uneven footsteps on the carpet soon revealed the cause of the panting. A little blond head came into view around the corner, and as my attention was drawn away from the computer screen, I met the most brilliant blue eyes. Two lips, wet with saliva, smiled wide and loudly said, "Hi!"

I couldn't help but smile and reply enthusiastically, "Hi!"

Bob came out of his office, "Dylan! Boy, am I happy to see you." Dylan launched himself at Bob's legs and grabbed on. I stood and came around the edge of the desk.

Bob introduced us, "Dylan, this is Miss Jessica. Miss Jessica, this is Dylan."

"I love you!" he said, slightly slurring his words.

Elizabeth came up beside me at that point, saying, "We're working on that." Before she could go on, the front door opened and Sabrina, Dylan's mom, came in with a CPS case aide. Elizabeth greeted Sabrina and said, "Dylan, look who's here."

"Mom! Hi, mom!" Dylan launched himself toward her. He wrapped his arms around her legs.

"Hi, Dylan," his mom replied, touching his head with her

hand. She kept her attention on Elizabeth. "Elizabeth, they won't let me …."

"Let's go into the conference room," Elizabeth cut in before Sabrina could continue. The case aide said he'd be waiting in the car and exited through the front door. Dylan grabbed his mom's hand, pulled her into the open conference room, and Elizabeth followed. I watched them enter, sounds from Dylan continuing as the door closed.

Bob stepped toward me and lowered his voice a little. "Dylan has some specific special needs. He doesn't have the normal boundaries that children his age might have. He hugs, kisses, and says I love you to almost anyone he meets."

I quickly understood. "Ah, I see. That's what Elizabeth was referring to working on?"

"That's right," Bob continued, "and there's more, but we won't go into that now." I returned to the computer to finish the emails and Bob returned to his office. A few minutes later I heard some commotion and Dylan's voice raise, then his mother's voice raise, and Elizabeth's voice, lower, cut in. I finished my work and headed out before their visit ended.

My mind wandered as I drove to my next appointment. It was Dylan inside my brain. I wondered what his story was, what the situation was. His mother's reaction to him made me feel a little sad and disappointed. I thought about how he had immediately gone to her and wrapped his arms around her legs. Her reaction to him was a quick response and a touch to the head. She didn't smile back at him, and she didn't seem particularly happy to see her child.

It was several months later that I transitioned from the Early Intervention program to the Developmental Home Program. When I received my assigned caseload, the Maxwells and Dylan were part of it. I was excited to recognize his name and looked forward to learning more about the child I had met previously.

CHAPTER 9

MONITORING FAMILY VISITS TURNED OUT to be more involved than I had anticipated. When I was assigned the case and learned about this additional task, I was a little excited. I was certain that my observation skills, something I prided myself on, would come in handy. I was certain that this would be a simple task to add to my workload. Typically, a social worker from Child Protective Services or the Division of Developmental Disabilities (DDD) would monitor family visits, but since the birth family lived so far away, the department only provided transportation for the visits and asked our agency to provide monitoring.

Visits began taking place at our office in the conference room. There was a long, solid table, several chairs and a mini kitchen. The conference room provided a more comfortable setting than an office, plus the sink and running water came in handy for washing hands and general clean-up.

When I began monitoring visits, I wondered why DDD wasn't monitoring them. They sent a case aide every week to drive the family there. Dylan's mom and siblings lived about four hours away. The licensing agency, my agency, was tasked with monitoring the family visits. I finally asked why and was told that though this was not typical we were doing our part to be supportive team members. Still a bit confused, I dove into my new role as visit monitor and got really good at documentation.

Soon after I took over as the licensing specialist, DDD found money to pay for a taxi service to drive Dylan's mom, Sabrina, and her other children there and back. The change occurred because Sabrina was pushing the case aides for information on her case, information about the foster family, and consistently asking for money for food for the kids. Often, she would convince the case aide to go through a drive-through and then say she had forgotten her wallet. The case manager and department supervisor finally decided to remove case aides altogether. Paying for a taxi service isn't typical. Government and State agencies often have very little budgetary wiggle room, but in this case it was deemed the best scenario and viewed as temporary.

When Dylan first went into Developmental Home Foster Care, he and his biological family had visits 1-2 times per month. Due to budgeting and scheduling constraints the visits decreased over the course of the year to once every 4-6 weeks. Sabrina agreed to the decrease. Time between visits also allowed Dylan more consistency in his routine.

Often during visits, Dylan's mom, Sabrina, would comment on the four-hour drive and how tired and hungry she or the kids were. She also stated several times how a visit day was basically ruined by six hours of travel time added to 1-2 hour family visit with Dylan. Everyone on Dylan's Child Family Team could empathize how difficult the experience must be for Sabrina and Dylan's siblings. However, we also knew how difficult the visits were for Dylan. Just a few hours off his routine could send him into a destructive spin. It wasn't just the difference in routine that affected him. The emotional toll interacting with his biological mother and siblings drained this small child so much that he had no ability to regulate himself in any way other than acting out.

Children are impulsive by nature. They have little capacity to think before acting. That skill is developed over time and gets stronger the older they become. When a child has a developmental disability or other type of disorder, the tendency toward impulsivity can be stronger and last longer because the capacity to reason, to think before acting, is less.

Behavior is a child's way of expressing their needs. I heard this once during a training on developmental disabilities. I have looked for the origin of this statement but have been unsuccessful. It is a simple, powerful, and perfect statement. When children act out, they aren't trying to ruin your day or the moment, they are simply expressing that they have a need and behavior is how they bring attention to it. Thought and reasoning do not factor into the equation.

For Dylan, a child with little-to-no impulse control in a predictable environment, any change to his routine stripped away feelings of security. The lack of security led Dylan to act out behaviorally. Some children might cry more, have sleepless nights, lose bladder control, hit, bite, or scream. Dylan exhibited all these behaviors, and even more destructive behaviors.

Ideally, when a child is placed into care outside of their home, family visits will take place at least once a week. Visits might take place in the family home, in the community, or at a designated Department of Economic Security facility. Both Child Protective Services and the Division of Developmental Disabilities fall under the umbrella of the Department of Economic Security. The Child Family Team (CFT), comprised of the biological parents, foster parents, Case Manager, Licensing Specialist, Therapists, and other specialists and people integral to the child's well-being, will meet regularly and determine the parameters of family visits. Often visits will be ordered by the court and the CFT will work to ensure the needs of the child are being met during visitations.

As the family visits continued, we began to see more characteristics of the home in which Dylan had been raised the first four years of his life. There was one incident that took place where Sabrina had asked for and accepted money from an employee at our office. She also asked the transport driver that day to buy food for her and the children on the way home. She told the driver she didn't have any money and that the children hadn't eaten all day. Hearing the story, I was dumbfounded and angry. It was clear, in my mind, that she couldn't provide for her children and the best place for Dylan was in foster care. In fact, the thought crossed my mind, that the other children would probably benefit from being in foster care, too. I was confused as to why Child Protective Services hadn't removed them from Sabrina's home yet despite having at least two reports to Child Protective Services. Still new to social work, I had a lot to learn.

Removing children from a home is not the goal of Child Protective Services, and it is not always the best option for the children and family. My personal feelings were based on relatively short observations from higher stress situations.

Soon a memo from the caseworker, David, was received. It stated that under no circumstances was money to be given to Sabrina. Transportation drivers would be notified before each pick-up that they were to not give any money. David shared that he had met with Sabrina and she understood this new rule. She was not to ask or imply that she needed money. This was difficult for many of us. Humans generally are kind and willing to offer help to someone in need. The type of people who go into social work or education careers often have a heightened desire to help others. The thought of someone going hungry can grip you to the core and cause you to dig out your last few dollars.

It's not that we were not caring. We would not want children or people to go hungry, but there were also allegations that the money was going to alcohol, cigarettes, lottery tickets, and possibly other substances. So, the owners of our agency, the director and I, discussed what we could do in the event that she asked for money for food. We settled on having food available and began providing peanut butter, jelly, and bread, and bottles of water. It was actually kind of nice because making sandwiches provided a bit of an activity for the family during the visits.

It was interesting when I observed them during these times. Often mom would make hers first, take a bite, and as she continued to eat hers, she made sandwiches for the two younger kids and Dylan, then she would push the bread, jelly, and peanut butter over to the oldest boy for him to make his own.

The family dynamics were painfully disjointed. It was clear to me that mom wanted someone to take care of her. It was clear she had unmet needs of her own.

CHAPTER 10

"I MAD AT YOU. I hate you!" he growled. It was dark out and I was a bit lost trying to take him back to his house. The directions that I had written down were of no help and I think I must have missed a road or something either in writing them down or I missed it while driving. I had pulled over to the side of the road on a neighborhood street and was trying to call Jane for directions to get to her house.

My work phone had one sporadic bar, indicating cell service that would flicker in and out. I pulled out my personal cell, which had service from a different carrier. I pushed a button and the screen lit up, only to show its 'No Service' notification. I tried to keep the nervousness and anxiousness out of my voice as I tried to reassure Dylan. He began kicking the back of the seat. "I understand that you are scared because I haven't gotten you home yet," I said. This was the second time I had driven him home. The first time it was still light out.

We were on the way home from a visit with Sabrina, Dylan's biological mom. She was alone this visit and the hour and a half felt like it dragged on forever. During most of the visit she wanted to talk with me about my life. Not wanting to ignore her, I shared tiny bits of information. And then I would redirect her attention to her son. Dylan was often running or stumbling around the office during visitations. My role during these visits was to observe and monitor the interactions between Dylan and his mom, and sometimes his siblings. I wasn't there to entertain or distract. More often than not, I was the one interacting with him, guiding him, playing with him. Sabrina would sit off to the side, ask an occasional question, and sometimes, play beside Dylan, but not play *with* him.

Visits happened once or twice a month. Dylan's routine would be interrupted. It often took a full two weeks before his behavior calmed down enough to a more manageable and predictable state. Then another visit would happen, and the cycle would begin once more. Dylan's behavior ranged from difficult to extreme. On a normal day, hitting, kicking, spitting, throwing, biting, and scratching might occur with periods of snuggles, laughter, and silliness. On a day with extreme behaviors he might exhibit the normal behaviors along with attempted strangulation, attempted stabbing, vomiting, fecal smearing, and full-body tantrums, just to name a few. The behaviors occurred all day long. It is very common for children, with or without special needs, to act out when their routines are disrupted. Consistency is key to helping a child feel secure. Unfortunately, in situations of foster care, predictable routines are difficult to maintain.

All the roads in this neighborhood wound around and twisted. The development was nestled at the base of one of the many mountain ranges in Maricopa County. The roads seemed to follow the pattern of the mountains. Some developers took advantage of this and liked to make these neighborhoods in more of a flowing pattern, not on grids, so that they could entice buyers with interesting layouts and scenic views. More artistic yes, but darned hard to find your way when you don't really know where you are going. Trying to write out directions using North, South, East, and West became very difficult. I crumpled up the directions I had written down. I picked up the phone again, praying for service and finally got two bars. I called Jane. She was almost as confused as I was but helped me get back to a main street. From there I made my way to the house. Two minutes later I parked in front of the house and turned off the car. Dylan had been screaming, growling, and kicking the back of my seat the whole time. As soon as I opened my car door, he sat up tall, with a smile on his face.

"We home, Skiska?"

I unbuckled Dylan and he ran to meet Jane, who was standing in the open front door. I could see Phillip walking toward the door, behind her. Through a front window, I could see the Maxwell kids bounding down the stairs as we neared the front door. Jane bent down toward Dylan and he launched into her, hugging and wiping his wet mouth on her shirt. I gave a quick rundown of the visit, highlighting some potential hiccups that might turn into difficult behaviors later. I shared Dylan's experience during our drive home as well. Jane had heard Dylan growling in the background over the phone when I called for help with directions.

One of my roles was to offer support and reassurance to foster families. This evening, Jane did that for me, in a reversal of roles. She smiled warmly, reassuring me that these things happen and that she would let me know how Dylan's behaviors were the following days.

CHAPTER 11

I SAID GOODNIGHT TO JANE and Phillip and waved to the kids. Dylan called out, "Skiska!" and gave me a tight squeeze around my legs. Cassie, the Maxwell's daughter, met me at the front door just as I opened it and gave me a hug, too. I stepped onto the patio and walked down the sidewalk to my car. The moon was bright and I could see right inside the car. Thirty minutes earlier the car felt like a prison. Now, it looked like the answer to my woes. It would take me home.

Finally on my way, I settled in for the drive. Geographically, I lived exactly opposite from the Maxwells. They lived in the Northwest area of the Phoenix valley and I lived in the Southeast area. At this time of evening the traffic flows pretty smoothly. It took me an hour to get home. I was there by 9 p.m. I was exhausted and felt like a failure. I had been listening to the radio on the way home, keeping my mind at bay. As soon as I walked through the doorway from the garage to the kitchen of my home my brain switched on and wouldn't stop. *Was it professional to get lost transporting a child?* I hadn't even known that transporting children in my car was a possibility. No one told me about this part of the job. *Did I even have the right insurance? Is it okay? Isn't there supposed to be some training? What if something happens? Who would be responsible? I would. I would be the one they came after if something happened. What if I couldn't work with kids anymore?*

My husband was in our home office, working on the computer. "You're finally home. Long day?"

The thoughts racing through my mind created a buzzing that filled my body. I felt angry and unappreciated. I responded,

"Yep." I wanted to sit down and share how the day had gone. I couldn't. I needed him to ask me to share. Like a bottle of wine, the cork needs to be removed before the contents can be experienced. I felt like a cork was stopping me from sharing, but I didn't know how to express it without feeling like I would totally unload on him. I decided to keep it in. "I'm going to get ready for bed," I said, leaving the room.

"Okay, I'll be in in a minute," he replied.

Washing my face, I felt a wave of guilt wash over me. I knew I had no right to be angry. My husband hadn't done anything. Why did I feel so angry at him? Was it him I was angry at? The thoughts flooded my mind. The anger rose and fell. By the time I was done brushing my teeth, I had gotten hold of the anger and had squashed the feeling.

All emotion safely stuffed and locked deep inside me, I turned off the bathroom light. As I climbed into bed, I checked my cell phone. No calls or texts. I plugged it in to charge, set the 5:30 a.m. alarm and shut off the light. My husband came in about 30 minutes later. We said goodnight to each other. I rolled over and stared into the darkness. Physically and emotionally exhausted, my brain seized the opportunity to have the stage all to itself. One by one, thought after thought lit up the night in my mind. This was going to take a while.

CHAPTER 12

THE THIRD VISIT I MONITORED was one I will never forget. The conference room was not available this day, so I took the family and Dylan into a small office near the front door. There was a desk, and four chairs. The sandwich items were on the corner of the desk and the oldest son immediately went for them and began making a sandwich.

"I want to do that," Sabrina whined. The boy continued making the sandwich as if he didn't hear her. Sabrina took a step toward her eldest child. The sound her hand made as she smacked the back of his head caught me off guard. I stood there stunned. The boy whipped around, facing his mother. His body was rigid, hands open but tense. I opened my mouth to say something, but nothing came out. "I told you, I want to make the food." Sabrina spit the words out. Her son took two quick steps toward a wall and flung himself into a sitting position against the wall. He pulled his knees up, glanced at me, then hid his face as he put his arms on his knees.

My heart was pounding, ears buzzing, and my face felt full of cotton. I stared at Sabrina and muttered, "Uh...." *What was I supposed to say? What am I supposed to do?* I knew it wasn't right. Striking a child was never okay. *How do I address this?* I'd never been in this position before. Up to this point I had spent more than ten years working with children and families in some capacity from education to social work. I had made reports to Child Protective Services before. I had never actually witnessed it myself. I was in charge. I was responsible. *How do I address this?* I racked my brain and tried to remember the guidelines for reporting.

I had seen children spanked in public. I had watched a parent grab a child by the upper arm to get their attention or pull them along. A slap against a child's head can be debatable as to whether it is abuse or not. In this situation it clearly warranted a report to Child Protective Services.

I muttered "Um," a little more loudly. I think Sabrina knew what she did wasn't okay. She avoided eye contact. "Sabrina…." I began.

She looked up quickly. "I know. You're gonna tell on me." She turned to her oldest son, still on the floor but now joking with his sister. "I'm sorry, okay?"

"Yeah, mom."

"Do you want them to take you away from me, too?"

"No," he said quietly.

I finally found my voice and said weakly, "Just like we tell the children to use their words when they're fighting, you can use your words…." Sabrina turned to look at Dylan who was chewing on the collar of his shirt, now drenched with saliva.

"Dylan. Get that out of your mouth." She glanced in my direction but didn't look at me. Dylan kept his shirt in his mouth. Sabrina had turned back to the peanut butter and jelly. Dylan bolted the few steps to where Sabrina was and grabbed a piece of bread with some peanut butter on it. "No!" Sabrina yelled at him, trying to pull the bread away. Dylan had stuffed three quarters of it in his mouth. She started to reach out for his arm, but he fell to his knees and began crawling away, dropping part of the bread on the carpeted floor, peanut-butter side down.

The rest of the visit continued this way, though there was no more physical punishment. Sabrina asked Dylan lots of questions. "How is school? Who is your teacher? Do you like this? Do you like that? What's my name? Do you love me?"

Many of these questions Dylan didn't or was unable to answer. To the question of "Do you love me?" Dylan readily replied, "I love you," and wrapped his arms around Sabrina's hips, burying his saliva covered mouth in her side.

"Ouch! You bit me!" Sabrina yelled, peeling Dylan off of her.

He smiled and made a laughing sound: "Heee, yeee, heee."

I decided to end the visit a little early at just under an hour. As soon as Sabrina and her other children were on their way, I called Jane's cell phone to let her know the visit ended early and she could pick up Dylan. After hanging up with Jane, I played with Dylan on the floor of the office, avoiding the peanut butter smear on the carpet.

Jane arrived and I gave her an overview of the visit. Once she left with Dylan, I set to work on the peanut butter-stained carpet and used the time to wrap my brain around the incident of Sabrina smacking her son's head. I also needed the time to calm myself. Once I was finished with the carpet (the stain never fully came out) I called Dylan's case manager to report what I had seen. David, the case manager, stated that he would make the report to CPS for me if I wanted and that if they needed my statement, he would let me know. I thanked him for the offer and gladly took him up on it. The family had an open CPS case and David needed to update the CPS case manager on a few other things, so he would add this incident to his list.

CHAPTER 13

WHEN DYLAN ENTERED FOSTER CARE, it was immediately clear he would need specialized care that included therapy. Sometimes getting therapy approved can be difficult. Luckily for Dylan, David, the case manager, was on top of it and got it approved. Jane took Dylan to his first appointment within the first month of him joining the Maxwell home.

Therapy for children with traumatic experiences needs to be individualized and handled delicately. Sitting down and talking with a child isn't going to cut it. Therapists must first develop a relationship and build trust, just as the foster parents do. They must realize the child has experienced trauma in the home, then trauma in the removal from that home, and then next that trauma can be experienced moving into a foster-care situation. Different levels of trauma can be experienced at each new experience the child has.

The therapist assigned to Dylan had a special certification in Play Therapy and determined that would be the best starting place for Dylan. Play Therapy allows a child to explore and express themselves through toys, games, and activities that a therapist leads them through. For several weeks, Dylan, his therapist, and Jane came together and played. This allowed the therapist to build some continuity and develop a relationship with him. Toward the end of every session Jane and the therapist would step out of the therapy room while a therapy assistant joined Dylan. As Jane and the therapist watched Dylan through a two-way mirror, they would discuss Dylan's actions and behaviors, his interactions with others, and other areas of concern. Through observation and information gathered through the sessions, the therapist and Dylan's psychiatrist were able to diagnose Dylan with Reactive Attachment Disorder and Mild Mental Retardation (the term accepted at the completion of this book is Intellectual Disability).

According to the website www.attachment.org, Reactive Attachment Disorder (RAD) is defined as:

> *"...a complex psychiatric illness that can affect young children. It is characterized by serious problems in emotional attachments to others. RAD usually presents by age 5, but a parent, caregiver, or physician may notice that a child has problems with emotional attachment by their first birthday.*
>
> *Symptoms of RAD include: detached and unresponsive behavior; difficulty being comforted; preoccupied and/or defiant behavior; disinhibition or inappropriate familiarity or closeness with strangers."*

The therapy sessions were intensive. Sometimes they lasted only 15-20 minutes and sometimes up to an hour. The length of time really depended on how Dylan was receiving the interaction.

Once Dylan seemed to settle into the routine of therapy, the therapist began to add experiences with Jane that would help build Dylan's capability to bond. The experiences were similar to what a parent would do with a baby such as spoon-feeding, bathing, and dressing. Bathing and dressing took place in the home, but feeding could be done during therapy sessions. The therapist also instructed Jane to cuddle Dylan in a blanket and rock him in a rocking chair while singing or talking to him. They continued with these activities for several weeks.

It was important to give Dylan these experiences, experiences he had not had as an infant with his own mother. The lack of early bonding and care can lead children to develop social emotional delays. RAD is an extreme form of this.

The activities helped develop a bond between Dylan and his foster mom. He began to call her "Mom."

It is natural for a foster child to call a foster parent 'mom' or 'dad', especially when there are other children in the home using those terms. This can be difficult for a biological parent to hear, however, and can cause anger, jealousy, and sadness.

Once, during a visit with his birthmother, Sabrina, Dylan referred to Jane as "Mom." Sabrina became angry. She grabbed him by the arm and made him look at her. "She is not your mom. Does she make you say that?" Dylan wriggled away and struck out at her with his arm, missing her. He ran to some toys and it was like she wasn't even in the room as he didn't acknowledge her the rest of the visit even though she tried to interact with him.

I explained to Sabrina that he was only copying what the foster siblings were doing. It was natural that he was calling Jane "Mom," too. She was very upset and told him not to call Jane "mom". That she was his only mom. He was confused and immediately began acting out, throwing toys and spitting. In the following week at home, Dylan had more tantrums than usual. One afternoon, after he had gone to the bathroom, Jane went to see if it needed any cleaning and discovered feces smeared on the wall and floor.

Fecal smearing has many causes. Behaviorally, it likely gave Dylan a sense of control in some way. Visits with his birth mother and siblings left Dylan feeling uncertain, anxious, and out of control. He acted out as a way to gain control and at the same time he had no control of his behaviors. He was just a little kid expressing himself.

Even though he felt anxious during and after visits, it didn't mean that he didn't love or want to be with them. It is common to care for someone and at the same time feel unsafe and unsecure with them.

Therapy was making a difference, but his behaviors continued to escalate, depending on birth family visits or how things at school were going.

One behavior that confused and sometimes delighted others was when Dylan would run up to a person, tightly wrap his arms around them and say, "I love you!" This was often accompanied with a slobbery kiss and more hugging. To see this small, beautiful child run up to you and announce his love was adorable. Except, in reality, it wasn't. It was a factor of his Reactive Attachment Disorder. Because of the neglect and lack of bonding in his first four years of life, he developed behaviors that were the opposite of what they should be. It is not a safe or healthy behavior to engage with unfamiliar people in this way.

Dylan's Child Family Team identified a list of people who were safe for him to engage in this way with. We then developed a plan of how to modify his behavior when out in public. It would take a lot of time and energy, but that was what it took to be a part of Dylan's team.

CHAPTER 14

I REMEMBER ONE DAY IN the office. I was still in the Early Intervention program and had met Dylan only once. It was late afternoon and Elizabeth, Dylan's first licensing specialist, entered flushed and agitated.

"Oh, my goodness…." she started.

"Are you alright?" a coworker asked.

"You don't know what just happened. After Dylan's visit with his mom, I buckled him into the backseat of my car. He was in such a good mood. As I shut the door, he reached up and his hand got shut in the car door!"

Tears started to fill her eyes. "Oh no," we said in unison. "Is he alright? Was anything broken?"

"No, no, I don't think anything was broken. There was just a little redness and no swelling. But I didn't realize it for a few seconds."

"Didn't he cry out?" someone asked.

"No," she said. "He just started laughing at me through the window and his face was turning red. He had the biggest smile on his face and that's when I saw where his hand was. I opened the door and he just kept smiling and laughing. He said something but I couldn't make it out, it was gibberish. I checked his hand and fingers. He moved them fine. I'm going to write a report to document it and submit it. When I took him home, Jane said she'd keep an eye on his fingers and let me know. He acted like nothing had happened and used his hand like normal. It was like he was backwards. His reaction was the opposite of what it should be."

This was concerning, to be sure. At his next therapy appointment Jane discussed it with the therapist, who said it wouldn't be unusual for Dylan to display mixed signals as a child with Reactive Attachment Disorder. She said that one visible sign of progress would be when he actually displayed appropriate responses to being hurt, sad, etc...

This came sooner than I realized. Two years after the car-door incident, I found myself monitoring a visit with Dylan and his birth family at a visitation facility in downtown Phoenix. The facility was very nice. It had been used at one time as a wing of a church. The church still operated on the East side and the West side originally had classes, a kitchen, offices, sports, etc. The church had kept ownership and offered the West wing of the building to the community. It had a gymnasium, an art room, kitchen, playground, and a few rooms set up like large living rooms with couches, tables, chairs, books, games, and toys.

We chose to use this facility because it was kept clean, had lots of space and lots of materials to use. When Dylan's mom and his siblings visited, this facility gave everyone plenty of choices for activities. On this day, Dylan's brother and sister wanted to play outside but the weather wasn't cooperating, so we headed to the top floor, to the gymnasium. There were basketball hoops, balls, jump ropes, Hula-Hoops, and other equipment for group play. Dylan's brother and sister were shooting baskets, Sabrina went straight for a chair. Dylan sort of wandered around. "Can we use those?" Dylan's sister asked me, pointing to some ribbon sticks that were out of reach. I said yes and went to get a few down. I grabbed some and as I turned, I saw Dylan. He had pulled a kid's chair (about 12 inches from the ground) away from the wall where his mother sat. He was attempting to stand on the chair.

His mom whined, "Dylan, get down from there."

I called to her, "Sabrina, can you go to him, help him down?" His balance was not very good. He had gotten all the way up now and was smiling, saying "Look at me, look at me."

Sabrina looked at me and repeated in an angry voice, "Get down. Jessica's going to get mad at you and you'll be in trouble."

"Can you help him down?" I asked again, making my way to him as fast as I could. I was at the half-court line, starting to jog over to them.

Dylan continued to smile and said, "Look at me!" He was delighted. "Jump!" he said.

I yelled "No, stop!"

But he had already stepped off. He fell like a tree, his face hitting the floor, straight on. He pushed himself up a little and there was blood and saliva trailing from his mouth. Stunned, he looked at the floor where some of the blood had dripped. He started breathing heavily and a whining, strangled cry came from his lips. I was on the floor with him by then. He looked at me, eyes glistening with tears as he wailed, "Ooowww!"

"I know, let me see," I cooed to him, hoping to soothe him. I checked his face and mouth. His top lip was beginning to swell, and he had broken a front tooth (not the first time). He threw himself at me and smeared his face on my shirt, climbing into my lap. My eyes started to well up and I choked back the building sob in my chest and throat. And yet, amid all the chaos of the moment, it was not lost on me that Dylan was feeling pain. He had never before cried or reacted appropriately in response to an injury.

My face was hot. I was pissed off at his birth mother who had approached us.

"I told you, you would get hurt, Dylan," scolded Sabrina.

"Sabrina, the visit is going to have to end now. He needs to see the doctor." She sighed and rolled her eyes, barely hiding her anger. "We've only been here thirty minutes. I'm supposed to get two hours."

"I know but we can't change what happened and he has to be taken care of. You will want to call your taxi now."

The siblings were upset about the short visit, but they were sad that Dylan was hurt and asked me if he was going to be okay. "I think so," I said. We said our good-byes and called Jane from the car.

We met at an Urgent Care, near their house. Dylan was acting mostly normal, and kept feeling the broken tooth with his finger. "It broken?"

"Yes, it broke again." He didn't seem to be in any more pain. The initial shock had worn off and he was back to normal. Jane took one look and said she was thankful that it was the tooth that had already been broken once. I asked if she wanted me to stay with her, and she said no, that she'd fill me in later.

She called me later that evening and said all was well. He had cut the inside of his lip, but not enough for stitches. And the broken tooth would be examined by the dentist the next day. I asked her how he was doing. She said he had his normal energy but was less aggressive.

CHAPTER 15

ONE DAY ABOUT THREE WEEKS after the car-door incident, Jane was taking the kids to the zoo. She had received a complimentary family pass from the therapist. It was October. Dylan had been with the family for a couple of years and was nearing his 7th birthday. The children were on fall break for two weeks, and Jane was trying to fill each day with an activity that the children would enjoy and would get them out of the house. The zoo pass came at the perfect time.

Breaks from school were both a blessing and a curse. The daily schedule and routine were changed. Children didn't have to get up at a certain time to get to school and the days were full of leisure activities and outings. The family still maintained a predictable time schedule for meals and bedtime, but sometimes lunch was a picnic at the park or dinner was eaten in front of the television for a family movie night. Disruption of the regular daily routine caused Dylan to lose predictability and structure, and thus made him feel unsafe. His behaviors always increased during times of change and unpredictability.

Jane struggled with Dylan's need for structure and predictability and her biological children's needs for variety and new experiences. Dylan benefitted from those things too, but at this stage of his development the benefit didn't quite outweigh the cost.

Ready for the zoo, Jane loaded the children into the minivan. Cassie, 6, and Jonathan, almost 5, sat in the middle row. Tyler, 10, sat in the third row with Dylan, now 7. The van was abuzz with the children talking about the zoo and the animals they wanted to see first. Dylan was smiling and growling a little. Dylan often growled when he felt uncomfortable.

Within the first few months of having Dylan placed in the Maxwell's foster home, the family made some adjustments. They realized that Dylan couldn't sit in the middle row of the minivan. Safety was the main focus. He was too close to the driver and could bend and stretch his body to interfere. He could kick out his legs and strike the driver and the passenger. The last row was safest. It was also decided that he would have that row to himself. With another person sitting in the back with Dylan, it was too easy for him to reach out and hit, scratch, bite, or pinch them. Often, when the whole family was on an outing, Mr. Maxwell or Jane would sit in the back-row seat with Dylan. They could help control his behaviors and also help him to feel less alone.

The first 20 minutes of the drive were uneventful. Jane had just entered onto the 101 freeway when she heard Tyler say, "Stop. Dylan, don't do that."

"What's going on back there?" Jane asked as she glanced in the rearview mirror. She saw clearly what was going on. Dylan had hold of his unbuckled seatbelt and was stretching it forward. He then put it around his younger foster brother's neck and pulled back on it, effectively strangling the boy. "Stop, Dylan!!" Jane yelled, pulling to a stop on the freeway as far to the side of the road as she could. She scrambled out of her seat and attended to her son. His face was red, tears rolling down his cheeks as he cried and coughed.

Dylan was smiling and repeatedly saying "Hi, mom, I love you."

Jane, in her calmest voice, replied, "Dylan, you can use your words to get my attention. We don't hurt others." She switched the seating, putting the two younger siblings in the back row with Tyler and Dylan alone in the middle. She suspected that Dylan was attempting to get her attention and by putting him closer to her he might be able to reset himself for the duration of the car ride. Jane told him she wanted him to be closer to her.

"I'm closer to you, mom?"

"Yes, Dylan, I want you to be closer to me."

For the remainder of the ride, Jane was intent on distracting Dylan and there were no more incidents other than him taking his shoes off and continually unbuckling and buckling his seatbelt.

CHAPTER 16

WITHIN THE FIRST FEW MONTHS of Dylan's placement with the Maxwells he began seeing a psychiatrist. Jane Maxwell and Elizabeth, Dylan's first licensing specialist, had documented and reported his wide array of behaviors and developmental progress. At almost five-years-old, physically he was small for his age, very unsteady with frequent falls and trips every day, and his fine motor skills seemed to be sporadically uncoordinated. He constantly had his shirt or some other object in his mouth, gnawing. He seemed to produce an abnormal amount of saliva. He also had significant speech delays. He stuffed food into his mouth and gagged at almost every meal. He was unable to follow two-step directions, and often needed simple instructions repeated and modeled for him. He was distracted easily, but what child isn't? Yet Dylan's level of distraction was comparatively close to that of an 18-month-old.

To say he was hyperactive would be an accurate statement. Dylan ricocheted from one space to another, from toy to toy, person to person. Jane wondered if Dylan had Attention Deficit Hyperactivity Disorder (ADHD) or something else that would cause his extreme behaviors, other than the trauma he experienced in his first four years of life. She had talked with his teacher and the teacher suggested that he might have an attention disorder and that he might benefit from seeing a doctor about it.

Jane contacted Dylan's case manager, David, and shared her concerns and thoughts. David had already identified a potential psychiatrist to connect with. The psychiatrist was one that Dylan's therapist and his pediatrician often worked in partnership. David, having worked in the field for several years, knew it was a good idea to have a variety of specialists identified as a way of speeding up referrals and getting children's needs met in a timely manner.

Jane and Dylan met Dr. Barns on a Wednesday morning, and 30 minutes later they left with a prescription for a medication commonly used to treat ADHD. At the time, there were few studies and guidelines for treating children as young as five years old. Dylan's psychiatrist was not ready to diagnose Dylan with an attention disorder but felt medication may make a difference and even be able to offer some insight.

After five weeks, it was clear the medication was not making any difference. The dosage was increased, and two more months later Dr. Barns decided to try another medication. The new medication seemed to put a dent into the hyperactive tendencies of Dylan. Jane was feeling some relief but wasn't convinced that it was solely the medication. She, along with his therapist, felt that some of his improvements were also due to the stability in his life, as well as therapy.

Another five months passed when Jane began to notice that Dylan's high production of saliva began to increase. She brought it up to the psychiatrist and Dr. Barns identified that Dylan was drooling. Because Dylan had been seeing a speech and feeding therapist and had made improvement to his oral motor muscles, he felt that the drooling might be a side effect of the medication.

A third medication was tried and after about six months, an appropriate dosage was settled on for Dylan. Dr. Barns had officially diagnosed Dylan with ADHD.

Anyone who met Dylan after he began medication would have never believed he was on anything to help him slow down and focus, because he was still an extremely busy and distractible child. Those who worked with him before the medication, and then after, noticed a difference. He was still

Dylan, but he was able to attend to tasks for sometimes more than five minutes.

Medication is not always the answer for children and adults with attention disorders. For many, dietary modifications, environmental adjustments, and behavioral supports are all that is needed to make significant improvements.

CHAPTER 17

WHEN DYLAN SMILED AT YOU, blue eyes sparkling, the corners of your mouth automatically curled up in response. It was inevitable. The desire others had to connect with him was strong. Today, he wrapped his arms around me and squeezed until my legs began to pulse with discomfort. "I yuv you, Skiska."

"I love you too, Dylan."

"Who's dat!" Dylan asked loudly, looking at a man in line beside us. Before I could answer, Dylan was lifting his arm in a wave. "Hi!" he exclaimed and let go of my legs. I quickly grasped one of his arms before he left my side. I was always on high alert with Dylan. He had a habit of running into parking lots and roads, out of rooms, and engaging unfamiliar people.

With people, whether he knew them or not, he would hug them, kiss them, hold their hands. The first time I met Dylan I experienced this interaction and thought how cute he was. Almost everyone thought so. Soon I was educated on how dangerous this behavior was to him and to his therapy progress.

Dylan's diagnosis of Reactive Attachment Disorder (RAD) mixed up his ability to bond, create relationships, and have healthy boundaries.

We were in McDonald's, waiting in line to order. The man he had become interested in was beside us. The man looked to be in his 50s with very dark, sun-tanned skin. He had deep lines in his face that deepened as he smiled down at Dylan. The man noticed my grip on Dylan's arm. He turned back to face the counter. My mind raced. *Did he think Dylan was my kid? Did he think I was afraid of him?* I wasn't, but outward appearance might have suggested another story. The blossoming embarrassment in my chest halted as it was our turn to order.

Often, after biological family visits, I would take Dylan to McDonald's before dropping him off at the Maxwells. It was his favorite place, and it was a useful carrot to dangle when attempting to get him in the car or distract him from other behaviors.

"Shigen nuggess!" Dylan exclaimed.

I ordered, then took the tray of chicken nuggets, French fries, ketchup, and box of apple juice to a nearby booth. I sat the tray down and helped Dylan climb into the booth, sliding along the molded plastic seat beside him, and mostly trapping him in. He reached for the fries and before I could stop him, shoved more than half of the small-sized order in his mouth. I anxiously watched and got a napkin ready. The cough erupted seconds later and I was able to catch most of the fries and saliva in the napkin. Dylan gagged loudly a couple of times, which caught the attention of a few nearby diners.

I quietly reminded Dylan about taking small bites and chewing. His hand shot out toward the chicken nuggets, but I was ready and grabbed his wrist before he could get a large nugget in his mouth. "Help me tear off a small piece for you, Dylan," I said.

His hand began to clench around the nugget, not letting up, and I pulled away most of it before letting his wrist go. In the mouth went his fingers along with the bit of nugget. As I coached him on chewing, I simultaneously tore the nuggets into small pieces, only putting two in front of him at a time. Both of his hands held nugget pieces, and both of my hands held his forearms. As soon as I could see him start to swallow, I let one arm go. This process slowed down his eating and helped him practice chewing. If he wasn't eating something like yogurt or pudding, he was spitting, gagging, and vomiting, unless someone was feeding him, as I basically was.

He finished the fries and nuggets. I handed him the bottle of apple juice after putting a straw in it. A straw helped slow his drinking, plus there was much less spilling with a straw, if he kept the container on the table. A straw also helped with oral motor development. It had taken Dylan quite a while to learn how to suck liquid through a straw. After blowing bubbles, then gulping his juice down and me chatting away, I took some clean napkins, got them a little wet with water from my water bottle and handed him some to wipe his face. When he had wiped and swiped at his mouth and cheeks I asked if I could help him, too. He said yes and I finished the clean-up. We got up to throw the trash away. I had the tray in one hand and his hand in the other.

Dylan pulled on my hand, leaning toward the counter. He was pointing at the menu, brightly lit overhead. I told him it was dinner time at home, and it was time to get back because Jane wanted to see him. She missed him and it was time to finish. I reminded him we only have one meal at McDonald's. Dylan very rarely stopped eating on his own, and only when the food ran out from his plate or from the table in front of him.

Dylan had to be closely monitored around food for both his physical and mental health. At home, this task fell mostly to Jane, making mealtimes stressful.

CHAPTER 18

"UGH, OWW, YUCK!" DYLAN WAS gasping and panting as he trudged up the bank from the pond. His soaked socks and shoes made slopping sounds on the damp ground. He was wet up to his knees. He was smiling and at the same time had an expression on his face of discomfort. "Hep me, hep!" He wiped his mouth with his hand that was wet from the pond water and spit when his wet hand swiped across his face. "Yuck," he said almost matter-of-factly. I stood looking at him, amazed in some ways, disheartened in others. "Hep me," he said again.

I was already moving forward, frustration building in my chest. Jaw clenched. I kept a calm look on my face as I moved forward to help him. He was slipping on the muddy slope at the bank, making it hard for him to climb up all the way. However, two steps to the right or left would have given his feet the ground, not wet, not muddy, to step on and gain purchase. Reaching my hand out to him, I directed, "Step this way, Dylan." He took half a step to the right and slipped down again, hands and knees in the mud now.

"Uh, Oh" he said. "Yuck, dirry."

"Yep," I replied, "Its okay. You will get cleaned up when we get you home."

"We going home?" he asked.

"Yes," I said.

"No!" he shouted.

I reached out my hand to him and he reached out to me. I grabbed his forearms with both of my hands and pulled him up. As I did so, he let his legs and then his body go limp so that I was dragging him through the mud.

"Dylan," I sighed out, "get your legs under you. I'm not going to drag you."

"Can't, can't," he smiled. I dragged him a few feet to some dry grass and let him down on the ground. "I'm wet," he said looking down at himself.

"Yes, you are," I replied. I scrambled in my mind for what I might have in the car that I could put under him in the seat. To the best of my knowledge, I still had an old blanket in the trunk. I kept hold of Dylan.

He'd started wailing at having to leave the park. "Sorry, I be good," he repeated. Over and over.

"Dylan, you are good." He began yanking his hand without releasing himself from my grasp. "Dylan, it's just time to go home. Jane is waiting for you."

"Mom? Mom Jane?" I saw his eyebrows raise.

"Yes, Mom Jane."

He frowned, "I hate mom."

"You hate mom?" I asked.

"I hate mom," He insisted. He wrenched his hand from mine and shoved me with both arms on one of my hips and took off running. For such a small boy he had a lot of strength. He was fast but he also had very poor balance and fell to the ground on his chest. I reached him as he righted himself and he came at me again. I put my palms down on his shoulders, putting pressure on his frame, my hands open, not squeezing, just pressing down.

I noticed that when he started to act in a violent way, he would begin to lose control and his body would act sporadically. I had learned in a training about kids with certain sensory needs that "grounding" them could help. When Dylan seemed to lose control of his body, I felt he needed some kind of input, some kind of stimulation to give him something to meet his needs. It sometimes helped to calm and slow his energy.

The hands on the shoulders worked enough for him to give up physically coming at me and shoving. Then he started spitting. "I hate you, I hate you," he said, spitting at me.

We started moving to the car, me behind him, hands on his shoulders gently pushing down while walking him forward, and him continuing to say terrible things. At the car I asked if he wanted to help me. "No!" he growled. I held his hand and popped the trunk, pulling out the blanket. I laid the blanket on the seat while he squirmed and pushed to get in the car.

He then pulled away from me and dropped to the ground. He scooped up some gravel and dropped it, then did it again and again. I got the blanket situated, then helped him stand, wiping the gravel off his hands. He climbed in chattering the whole time and asking, "What's this?"

"A rock."

"What's this?"

"Another rock...."

I'd learned to make sure his hands were empty before getting in the car, as well as his pockets and shoes. He climbed in and I buckled him in, made sure the child lock was on, his hands were away from the door (he was taking off his shoes), then shut the door.

I quickly got to the driver's side and got in, reaching immediately back to grab his shoes and socks that were now on the floor and seat, putting them on the floor in the front while cheerfully chatting away, trying to distract him from me removing the shoes and socks, as they were potential items he could throw out the window as we headed to his home. He caught on as I grabbed the last sock and I changed my voice to a higher pitch and asked excitedly, "Should we call Mom Jane?"

"I want to call Mom Jane!" he hollered.

"Okay, let me get the phone out." I dialed and put the sound on speaker. When Jane didn't answer I left a message that we were on our way home and should be there in about 15 minutes.

"I want to talk to Jane!" he called out again and again.

Each time I replied "I know you want to talk to her. She didn't answer the phone, so we left her a message."

"I want to talk to her. Call her!"

"When you talk to Jane," I cut in, trying to direct him, "What will you say to her?"

This stopped him for a moment, and he smiled. "I love you. I love you, Mom Jane." His face had turned gushy sweet, and a big smile took over. "I hate mom. Dinner?"

"You'll ask her what's for dinner, or are you hungry?"

"I'm hungry. We going McDonalds, Skiska?"

"You like McDonalds, don't you?"

"McDonalds!" he cheered loudly.

"I like McDonalds, too. We aren't going today, Dylan. We have to get you home for dinner."

"We going McDonalds?" he asked again.

"We're going home today, but next time we are going to McDonalds. This time we are going home to Mom Jane."

"We going to McDonalds?"

"Dylan, we're going home."

"I want McDonalds! I hate you." Splbbbbthbthbb... the spitting began again.

"Let's sing a song. You love Old MacDonald. Old MacDonald had a farm, EIEIO..."

He chimes in on the EIEIO loudly. "On his farm he had a Dog," shouts Dylan. "EIEIO!" We get to the second woof woof and he's back on McDonalds. Perhaps it was my choice of song. He repeats the questions again and again and I repeat my answers again and again, trying every few questions to get on a new topic, with no luck.

CHAPTER 19

FINALLY, WE PULL INTO HIS neighborhood and I say, "Dylan, do you recognize anything?"

"What?"

"Do any of these houses look familiar?"

"My house!"

"That one looks similar to yours, but it's not. We're getting closer to your house."

"Jane!" he shouts from the back seat.

We pull up to his house and Jane opens the front door. I turn off the car and Dylan's yanking on the door handle trying to open the door as I open mine. "Remember, I need to open it from the outside. Try to get your seatbelt unbuckled." He turns his attention to the buckle. About 60 percent of the time he can get out with no problem, the other 40 percent it's like he's never unbuckled a seatbelt before and needs an adult to help him. Today he's having trouble and is pulling on the seatbelt, clawing at it and pulling it tighter around his body.

"Hep me hep me!" He starts to growl and saliva trickles down his chin.

I open the door and reach through to unbuckle him. Once free he says, "Awww, Skiska, I love you." Then he sees Jane and is frantic to get to her. He jumps out of the car barefoot and beelines for Jane.

"Oh my," she says, "look at your pants."

"He's been on a bird-catching expedition," I say.

Jane smiles at Dylan and says, "Let's go in and get you cleaned up."

"Okay, mom. I love you," He says, leaning into her, hugging her leg tight and kissing the side of her thigh. I follow them in, carrying his socks, shoes and backpack. Jane takes him upstairs and I drop the shoes and socks in the laundry room before heading to the living room to wait.

Two of the family's children were in the living room reading books, the oldest child was in the kitchen doing homework. As soon as I sat down the daughter snuggled up to me and put a book in my lap. "Will you read this to me?"

"Of course," I say and open the book.

Her brother, the youngest of the family, around four years old, joins his sister and we read the book until we hear footsteps pounding down the stairs and Jane's voice calling, "Slow down, Dylan."

Dylan bounds into the living room, sees us, makes a beeline and grabs the book from my hands and flings it across the room with a huge smile on his face. He squeals "Skiska!" and buries his face in my lap.

"Hey!" The two other children call as the book slides across the room.

Dylan turns his face to them, grabs the sister's shirt with his hand, pulls on it as she whines and begins to scream at him. His fist clenched in the shirt, my hand immediately over his trying to calm him and not let him pull the shirt enough to hurt her, he's looking at her, his eyes wild, teeth clenched, saliva trickling out the corners of his mouth and face turning red.

"Stop it, stop it!" the girl screams.

"Dylan," I say, "let's find something for you to grab on to."

As I say this he turns from where we are and runs into the kitchen. Jane makes it to the bottom of the stairs and immediately Dylan barrels into her as the two children in the living room start with, "Moooom, Dylan threw our book...."

Dylan rebounds off of her, runs into the playroom and begins to rummage around in the toys. Jane replies to the children, "I know he threw your book. Do you remember we talked about how he feels when he comes home from visiting with his birth mom?"

"Yes," the daughter replies.

Jane continues, "You might want to go play in your room until dinner."

"Okay, mom." The children go upstairs.

Dylan hears their footsteps and starts toward the stairs but Jane calls to him and he's redirected for a moment. He runs to her and snuggles into her arms, then bounces out and back into the playroom where he begins to bang on some plastic tubs the kids use as drums.

Jane leans back on the couch, sighs and looks at me. "So, how was it today?"

I smile and said, "It was like most of the visits. She didn't spend much time with Dylan except to watch him and holler at him. She hugged him at the beginning and end, though he clearly didn't want to at the end. He was ignoring her, and she kept looking to me and asking me to make him come to her. I explained that it often helps to go to him instead of asking him to come to you. She didn't budge."

Jane cut in, "I think she's afraid of him."

I reply, "I think she's on edge because she's not alone with the children, I'm watching and really I don't think she knows what to do with them. When she gets down to play with them, it's more like I'm watching a big kid play. She doesn't engage with Dylan or the other children, she just plays beside them. I'm still trying to model for her healthy ways to play with the kids but when I'm near she just asks me questions about my life."

"Did she ask you about us again?" Jane asks.

"No. Not today."

The last visit, Sabrina had asked so many questions about the foster family. I couldn't answer any of the questions except for vaguely.

"I think she's worried about being judged," says Jane.

"Of course she is, and she is being monitored. It can't be comfortable for her." I state.

"Well, luckily today nothing major happened. She yelled at the kids a few times. Dylan and his older brother really seemed to play well for a longer period of time this visit. The brother seemed to have more patience. The sister had less interaction, but that's normal. There was no hitting or pushing this time with any of the kids or mom.

"After the visit Dylan and I stayed at the park because he was so attracted to the birds and was chasing them. That's how he came to be wet and muddy. There were a couple of ducks near the water, and he was able to get pretty close to them before they escaped onto the water and paddled off. Dylan had been approaching them by moving down a little hill and as the ducks moved into the water, he moved a little faster and then the momentum just carried him into the water."

I started laughing as I said these last words. "I don't think he could have stopped himself even if he tried. I just sat there watching him. There's about 10 feet of super shallow water no more than a few inches deep. He was safe and was having so much fun. I felt like he needed to run off some of the energy from the visit. I just wish he hadn't gotten soaked so early. I would have let him keep running around, but I could tell he was uncomfortable in those wet clothes."

"Yeah," Jane says. "He has a really hard time with wet clothes. It's funny, he doesn't mind having stuff all over his face or hands or on his skin really, but when he is in wet clothes, he really can't stand it. When he wets his pants, or spills a drink on himself, or you know how he drools so much and sucks on the collar of his shirt? When the shirt touches his skin again, all wet, he gets very agitated."

I ask if it is worth talking with the therapist about. Jane doesn't think so because he is fine with the messy stuff and really it doesn't disrupt his day often or too much. As long as Jane makes sure to pack extra clothes in his backpack or have an extra set or two in the van when the family is out and about, it's fine.

"Jessica," Jane starts. "I am wondering about his excessive saliva. His mouth is always wet, more than when he first came."

We talk about the change and how long it's been going on. I say, "You know, Dr. Springer put him on a stronger medication, a little higher dose about six months ago."

Jane said, "But it didn't affect his drooling right away, so is it that?"

I reply, "It might be. Some meds just have to be in the body longer before you see the effects adverse or otherwise."

"I suppose so," she says.

I ask if she's noticed a behavioral difference between his lower dose and the higher dose.

"Not really. For the first three or four weeks, I noticed changes," she said, "but nothing that really lessened the severity of his behaviors."

"So, would you say he is the same, better, or worse behavior-wise on this higher dose?"

She says, "The same, but now he drools more." I tell her this is concerning and that she needs to contact Dr. Springer for a follow-up as soon as possible.

"Well, we have a visit next Monday," she says.

I say that's good, but that she needs to call the doctor ahead of time. Because he may need to plan for a longer visit than just a 15-minute medication review. I remind her that none of the meds he's been on are meant for kids as young as him and that the doctor is really just testing them out on him.

"I know. But, Jessica, he's just so hard to handle, I feel guilty, but I feel like if there was something to just calm him down a little. Not make him tired or sleepy or not himself, but less aggressive, less dangerous, less anxious."

"You've noticed a difference from when he first came to you and now, with the therapy haven't you? Remember when he was here only a month?"

"Oh my goodness, Jessica, I was ready to give up. Especially after he tried to stab the cat with the fork. He tried it so many times. We still don't keep the silverware accessible. It was like he was a feral animal."

I nod to her, remembering the stories.

CHAPTER 20

BEING A LICENSING SPECIALIST FOR a foster family with a kiddo like Dylan was full of twists, turns, and mountains of paperwork. I had to conduct twice-monthly monitoring visits, make sure the family was up to date on certifications, training, and home inspections. I also was responsible for maintaining documentation and communication between the dentist, medical doctor, psychiatrist, therapists, case manager, and submit details to the Foster Care Review Board (FCRB) as well as attend FCRB meetings and Child Family Team meetings. The Maxwells were not the only Developmental Foster Home on my caseload. There were 12 foster homes with placements and another seven homes that were licensed and awaiting foster placements. Of the 12 homes, five were Child Developmental Foster Homes and seven were Adult Developmental Foster Homes.

Developmental Foster Homes are similar to typical foster homes in that a foster parent or parents goes through training and obtains a license to provide care for a child or children needing care outside of their own home. Foster parents wanting to obtain a Developmental license go through significantly more training and preparation in order to provide care to a child.

One Saturday, I was on a hike with my husband. We chose to visit South Mountain in Phoenix, the nation's largest municipal park, with 50 miles of trails. As we navigated the dry, rocky trails lined with cactus, my thoughts were on Dylan and my work in foster care. The hike was difficult at times as we climbed higher and our breathing became heavier, hearts pounding with increased exertion. My mind quieted as my body worked. It was challenging, navigating rocks and dusty, slippery sloping trails. It was hot under the shining sun, and our bodies expelled sweat. The pressure of continuing on for our physical and mental benefit, for our accomplishment, felt heavy.

Each break we took to slow our breathing and gulp down water gave us the chance to look around and admire the sprawling landscape. The land, rising and falling in both smooth waves and jagged textures, was beautiful. Each saguaro standing tall reminded me of sentries guarding the land.

Without warning last week's visitation popped into my head, distracting me from the desert around me. Remembering the way Sabrina interacted with Dylan filled me with disgust and my mouth turned down as if I had tasted something unpleasant. At that moment I felt like I was with Dylan every day in some way. He was in my head. He lived with me in my home, he rode with me in my car, he attended my family gatherings.

Separating work from personal life can be challenging for many people. I was good at many things, but this wasn't one of them.

CHAPTER 21

ON A TUESDAY MORNING, I answered my work cell phone to hear Dylan's case manager, David, on the other end. "Good morning, David," I said.

"Well good morning to you, Jessica. Sorry to call so early, but I have some news about Dylan's case. The Foster Care Review Board and DDD is going to recommend severance for Dylan. He's been in care for almost 4 years now. Sabrina has not been able to meet the expectations of the court, and in fact she hasn't made progress on any of her parental goals except for one and that progress is far below expectations. I've talked with her about this. We will be having a formal meeting with Sabrina, her attorney, and our office tomorrow. The severance hearing has been set for next month. We will need your agency to attend, and it will be necessary for Jane to attend, as well." Severance is the process of terminating parental rights.

I took down the details and called my supervisor Elizabeth first, then Jane.

Elizabeth met with the owners of our agency to discuss travel arrangements and the case needs. As Dylan's first licensing specialist and now as my supervisor, Elizabeth had been a constant member of the Child Family Team for Dylan's case since he came into care with our agency. It was decided that Elizabeth and I would attend the hearing, Jane would attend too, of course, and our agency would pay for her trip. We valued her role as a foster-care provider and felt that she went above and beyond every day for the care of Dylan, while maintaining a loving home environment for her family. It would put the family in a bit of hardship to have

Jane away from the home for a day and a half. Her husband, Phillip, planned to take off work the day of the hearing. The children were in school, but just having Jane away from the home changed the normal routine. A change to the normal routine often threw Dylan into turmoil. His feeling of security after being in the home for a few years was more stable, but there was always an underlying fragility. Changes to his daily routine or to the people in that routine caused that security to crack and his behaviors would increase and become more intense.

The hearing was scheduled for a Thursday morning at 8a.m. in Safford, about three hours East of Phoenix. We decided to leave late on Wednesday, after the children were home from school and settled. Jane had spent a few days preparing Dylan for her short absence. She didn't discuss the case with him, just what was immediately necessary for his understanding and current environment. The discussion of severance would be conducted with Dylan's therapist and the rest of the Child Family Team. Because of Dylan's cognitive abilities, information had to be presented in a way that he could understand, and it had to be presented multiple times as his understanding increased.

The day before the hearing, Elizabeth and I picked up Jane at her home around 4p.m. on Wednesday. During the drive we chatted about lighter subjects for the first hour before the conversation turned to Dylan and the hearing. When we arrived in Bullhead City, we drove to the courthouse first to get our bearings, then checked into the hotel. None of us was very hungry, and instead shared some snack bars before settling in for the night.

When we arrived at the courthouse the next morning we were greeted by David, Dylan's Case Manager. We then saw Sabrina and her attorney. Jane immediately approached her and gave her a hug. This wasn't their first meeting, but they hadn't spent much time together. Sabrina hugged her back and they talked a little before the hearing began.

There were some requests Dylan's mom bargained for before relinquishing her rights. She wanted to see Dylan one more time. She wanted transportation to Phoenix for her and her other children. She asked for money for food for that day and admission to a water park or to the zoo. Up to this point all her transportation had been covered. She also wanted a guarantee that Jane and Phillip would keep Dylan and adopt him. The court took a recess for Sabrina and Jane to talk.

Jane spent time with Sabrina and assured her that she loved Dylan and would only make decisions she felt were in his best interest. She was also clear that at that time she couldn't commit to adopting Dylan without talking with her husband and their children. She shared that they planned to continue caring for Dylan. Sabrina said that she understood. When the hearing reconvened, Sabrina was granted a final visit with Dylan for herself only, to a zoo for four hours. Transportation and lunch would be provided. Regarding Dylan's siblings, the court ordered that sibling visitations continue as long as it was in the best interest of the children and as long as the department could provide safe transportation.

The severance hearing began and ended within about two hours, including a couple of breaks. There were tears, frustrated faces, and finally expressions of sadness and relief on the faces of those exiting the court room. It was clear that Sabrina loved Dylan, which had never really been a question. She was just unable to provide a safe and developmentally appropriate home for him. It was questionable whether she could do that for her other three children, but it was up to CPS to monitor and make that decision.

Sabrina went from hating Jane three years earlier to appreciating her. Sabrina considered Jane a friend in some way. Maybe that made it a little easier for her to agree to severance of her parental rights.

The final visit came one week later.

CHAPTER 22

I PICKED UP DYLAN FOR the final visit with his mother. My stomach and chest had been fluttering with nerves as I drove to his house. No, it all began the evening before, as I prepared for the zoo. I packed extra water bottles, a first-aid kit, some granola bars and thin carrot sticks. I threw some sunscreen, a hat, and a bottle of bubbles in the bag as well.

On the drive to pick up Dylan, my mind raced. Would Sabrina be difficult today? Would she be able to say good-bye? Would she ask for help with the courts? The decision was final. Her rights were severed. Would she try and run off with him?

I would conduct the visit alone. Sabrina would arrive in a taxi, as she had for each regular visit the past year. Dylan and I would meet her at the gate to the zoo. I ran through what the day would look like as I neared the Maxwell home to pick up Dylan. My vision began to swim as tears filled my eyes. I was sad that a mother was going to have her last visit with her child. Regardless of the care or lack of care she provided, the danger she put him in or the abuse and neglect she perpetrated, she loved her child. It is hard to understand, but it is true.

On the way to the zoo, Dylan was oddly still and quieter than normal. He asked, "We going see mom?" several times. I stated that we were going to see his mom and that we were going to the zoo. "Zoo!" Dylan exclaimed and began to growl and roar then laugh at his impression of what I suspected was a lion.

The 20-minute drive to the zoo ended as I pulled into the parking lot. "We here?!" Dylan called out followed by "Mom?" I parked and helped him out of the back seat, holding his hand firmly as I popped the trunk and took out my backpack full of supplies. "I carry it!" Dylan yelled. I helped him put it on. Dylan took a few steps, then lost his balance and fell forward on his knees and one hand. I had ahold of the other hand and pulled up as he was going down. His knees were a little scraped and I pulled out some bandages and an antiseptic wipe.

When we got to the gate Sabrina was there waiting. "Hi, mom!" Dylan said as he stopped in front of her and growled. We entered the zoo. I rented a wagon and put my backpack in it. Dylan started to get in.

Sabrina yelled at him, "Dylan, NO! That's for babies." Dylan swung his arm at her.

I asked, "What do we want to see first? Lions? Monkeys...."

Sabrina immediately replied that she wanted to see the monkeys. Dylan was beginning to separate from us. I asked Sabrina if she wanted to hold his hand. She held her hand out to him without a word. He came closer to her and then said, "Ride!" as he approached the wagon. I suggested Sabrina pull the wagon for him. She sighed and took the handle. The next three hours and 45 minutes were mostly uneventful. I only had to chase Dylan twice, and bandage one more scrape. Sabrina seemed to attempt to talk to Dylan more, asking him, "See the bear?" "See the flamingo?" Dylan pointed at most of the animals and often repeated the names.

Toward the end of the visit, we sat to have lunch. Sabrina said, "Dylan, I'm not going to visit anymore. I love you."

Dylan responded, "You not visit, mom?"

"No, I can't come visit anymore. You're going to stay with Jane, okay?"

"Okay, mom. Mom Jane!"

Sabrina looked a little sad and at the same time determined. We finished eating, and she said, "Come on, let's go take our picture at the front." Dylan held her hand this time for a few minutes as I turned in the wagon. We exited the zoo and I asked Sabrina where she would like to have their picture taken. She chose a position, and Dylan followed her to a spot with small and large boulders. He immediately began attempting to climb them.

"Get down from there!" Sabrina said as she grabbed the upper part of Dylan's arm.

I stepped in and helped him down. "Here, Dylan, you stand on this little rock and mom can stand beside you."

"OKAY!" He said loudly. I took several pictures and promised to email them to Sabrina's current CPS case worker who would then print them and give them to Sabrina.

The taxi pulled up exactly on time and Sabrina bent down and said, "Dylan, I have to go, and I won't see you again. Can I have a hug?"

Dylan launched himself at her and grabbed on for a hug. "I love you, Mom!"

"I love you too, Dylan," Sabrina said as Dylan barreled into me and hollered, "McDonald's!"

CHAPTER 23

FIVE MONTHS AFTER DYLAN'S SEVERANCE I was conducting a regular monitoring visit with the Maxwells. Jane and I were sitting on the couch, wrapping up, when Jane shifted her position. "Jessica, I have some news to share. We're moving to Flagstaff." It came out a little too fast, like when you pour too much dressing on your salad because it comes out faster than you expected.

"That's great!" I respond. We had foster homes in the Flagstaff area as well, and the change wouldn't be too hard. Unless they didn't want to maintain their foster care license. "Do you still want to keep your license? And why are you moving?"

"Well, Phillip's company is transferring him to their office there and he's getting a promotion. He's pretty excited about it. And, yes, we still want to maintain our license."

There was more to it and I could tell she was holding something back, so I smiled and waited.

"The thing is, we feel like we've taken Dylan as far as we are meant to, and we'd like to find a new foster home for him." The words tumbled out quickly again. Too much ranch on the salad.

I couldn't help but raise my eyebrows in surprise. "Oh, okay. I understand." I felt the weight of this announcement crushing me.

Jane stated that the transfer would happen in three months, but that they still needed to sell their house and she said that transitioning Dylan was a priority so that if she needed to stay longer with the kids if it was in his best interest, she would.

I left the visit and called Elizabeth, my supervisor, who knew Dylan as well as I did. She said we could meet the next day and talk about potential families.

The following morning, we started by identifying potential families but really only one stood out as a potential. The Browns were a two-parent household with five children, two out of the house and two teens and one preteen at home. What made them unique was their determination, commitment to community, love, and that they had four boys and one girl. We hoped if anyone could withstand and absorb the behaviors of Dylan and not run away it would likely be this family. The family was less snuggly and a little more straight-to-the-point than the Maxwells were, but this might be what Dylan needed to continue in his progress and move closer toward the social skills he would need later in life.

We posed the potential placement to the Browns and they were delighted with the opportunity. We explained why we thought it would be a good fit and the commitment to therapy that would be required. The family agreed, and Christina Brown, Jane Maxwell, and I planned to meet with Dylan at a park the following week.

We were at the park for about 15 minutes, just so Christina could observe Dylan interact with Jane and get a feel for him. It was also an opportunity for him to potentially meet her, too. Nothing was brought up about a potential move, but Dylan was told that Jane was meeting with her friend Christina.

Dylan was always curious around new people and kept checking in with Jane as she talked with Christina. "Mom, I love you. Mom, I love you."

Christina and Jane exchanged phone numbers and set a time to meet again in a few days for a little longer. After the third visit, Jane told Dylan that he was going to go to Christina's after school for a couple of hours, just like when he went to Barb's, his respite worker. Jane explained that Barb couldn't help that day and so Christina was going to help. Dylan went to Christina's and all went pretty well, except he couldn't leave the family dog alone.

Christina was anxious to move things along, but we explained that the transition needed to be slow. She met with Jane and Dylan at his therapist's office for a session. This was when it was introduced that Christina was like Jane and she helped take care of children like Dylan. He was very insistent that he needed to stay with Mom Jane. Slowly, over the next two months more visits happened, and a date was set for Dylan to move to the Brown's home. It was also arranged that Jane would visit Dylan at the Brown's home a few times and then have phone calls with her after that.

The transition was hard on Dylan. He kept asking for Mom Jane and to go back home. He was never lied to. It was made clear that he had a new home and that he could still talk to Jane and see her sometimes. A photo album had been made for him when he entered care that had pictures of his biological mom and siblings, of the Maxwells and, of course, Dylan. Pictures were added of the Browns. Dylan's family was growing. This type of transition and situation would be difficult for any child, let alone a nine-year-old with a cognitive disability and attachment disorder.

CHAPTER 24

THERE WAS A BIT OF a honeymoon stage where a lot of Dylan's behaviors were very short and not very severe. The family felt heartened by this, and I told them how happy I was that they were having this experience. I also told them that his behaviors may escalate and to just be prepared and remain calm. They had received full details of his history and behaviors. Christina smiled at me and said okay. I got the feeling she didn't believe me.

A few weeks later I got a call around 9p.m. Christina was on the phone and sounded a little out of breath. "I'm sorry to call you so late, but it's Dylan."

"What is it, is he ok?" I asked.

"Oh yes, he's fine, but my boys aren't. After dinner, he went to their shared room and urinated all over the room. The furniture, the beds, the rug, their shoes ... it's everywhere. When one of the boys saw it and freaked out, Dylan started spitting and scratching. It's all under control now, but I needed to call you."

"I understand," I replied. "Is anyone hurt from the scratching?"

"No. But it's a mess. I think we're going to have to put him in his own room." This was something we discussed before he moved in, but they were sure he would be fine with the older boys.

"My daughter graduates from high school next month and then moves for college in July. We'll move him in her room then," stated Christina. I asked her to document everything and I would stop by the next day.

His behaviors continued to escalate one-by-one but could only be characterized as moderate. None escalated to extreme, and those that were severe were only occurring about once a week. This felt like progress compared to the past five years. He regularly displayed behaviors of hitting, kicking, spitting, and running away, but these were manageable. Considering he had only been potty-trained for a few years his toileting and self-care skills were coming along as well. He could do a pretty good job of brushing his teeth on his own. Things were settling down.

The Browns weren't fazed by much and the relationship they built with Dylan was steady, practical, and loving. For the next year my visits with Dylan and the Browns were pleasant. I looked forward to hearing about how stable his behaviors had been with only minor ups and downs.

CHAPTER 25

ONE DAY I GOT A call from Dylan's current Division of Developmental Disabilities case manager. He stated he was leaving, and another case manager had been assigned. My heart jumped. I hadn't gotten along very well with the current case worker, as he hadn't spent any time with Dylan and was fighting me on the weekly therapy visits, due to cost. It was only two weeks previously that I finally convinced the case manager to spend some time with Dylan and meet with the therapist. The case manager saw clearly how necessary therapy was and how high Dylan's needs were.

So, after what felt like a long battle and just when things were starting to settle, something came along and shook our world.

I got the new case manager's name, number, and email address and called her right away to introduce myself and invite her to one of my home visits so she could meet Dylan and the family. She wasn't in, so I left a message. Three days later I sent her an email (because somehow phone messages didn't always get to the person you left them for) relaying my earlier message. I got a reply to my email a few hours later. She said she had already been out to meet Dylan. She also said there was an adoptive family she wanted to place him with, and she would call me the next day to set it up. My skin tingled, as I was excited and also worried. If she had met Dylan and read his file, she would know his needs. Wouldn't she?

She called the next day and stated that she had transferred over from an adoption unit and thought that the length of time for Dylan to have been in foster care was too long, especially at his age. He had all the qualities of a typically desired child. I was pleased to hear this from her, but there was apprehension in my gut.

Then she said it, "So I just have one question for you."

"Okay," I replied.

"Is he adoptable?"

The instant heat that washed over my body and my face made me uncomfortable. "Adoptable?" I almost laughed back into the phone. "I believe every child is adoptable, you just have to find the right fit for the child and family."

"Yeah, yeah, I know. You have to say that."

No, I don't, I thought, *it's the truth.*

"Just tell me if he is adoptable."

I said, in a very calm voice, though my blood was boiling. "Yes, Dylan is adoptable. To the right family."

But as I said that last sentence, she began talking over me. "He is cute, blond hair, blue eyes. The family I have in mind is looking just for a boy his age and would fit in perfectly with the family."

I knew she meant looks-wise, Christmas card-wise. I cut in as gently as I could. "Is the family trained to work with children with developmental disabilities?"

She said, "They're open to it, just not physical disabilities."

"He does have some balance issues sometimes," I blurted.

"That's not a problem," she said. I begin to explain the success we've had with the slow transition from his former foster home to the current one. I stressed the need for a slow transition and stated that the therapist recommends it.

"Yeah, we're not going to move him without meeting the family first. I was thinking of a visit this weekend."

My heart pounded painfully in my chest. "This weekend, like for a couple of hours?"

"No, from Friday to Sunday."

"No meet-and-greet first?" I was going into shock, I feel the numbness filling my feet; my fingers begin to lose feeling, too.

The case manager said she had to go, and the other family's agency is going to call and set things up with me. Then she hung up.

I felt as if I were flipping out, trying to keep my breathing steady. She had no idea what this might do, how far it might set him back. She's not the one who would have to live with him if this goes bad. And, poor Dylan, his little world is just starting to make sense again. Every change in his life, from getting a new backpack to being in a new environment, is a hurdle for him. It sends his body and brain into a buzzing ball of anxiety, energy, and often aggression.

Tears started to fill my eyes and I tried to work out who to call: his therapist, his foster mom, Christina, my supervisor, Elizabeth? I picked up the phone to dial Christina just to give her a heads-up, but the phone rang in my hand. It's a number I didn't recognize. I answer and heard a somewhat familiar voice, but I couldn't place the person.

"Jessicaaaa... this is Alexis with Alliance." Alliance was another foster care agency in Phoenix. Before working for Alliance, Alexis had worked for my agency, Child Connections. I met her briefly when I joined the agency, right before she quit to work for Alliance.

"Hi, Alexis, how are you?"

"I'm good, thanks. Listen, I want to let you know that I have a family that is interested in Dylan."

"Oh? That's interesting. I just spoke with his new case manager and she also mentioned a family interested in him."

"Yeah, that's my family. Listen, we've already talked about him and I think this weekend is going to be the best time to get a visit in."

"Alexis, is this family aware of Dylan's needs? Are you aware of Dylan's needs?"

"Jessica..." she says with a condescending tone, "I know Dylan. I knew him before you did. He's going to be fine. This is going to work out for everyone."

"Alexis, I don't think this is a good idea. I know you used

to work for my agency and met him before, but that was years ago. Dylan can't move quickly without damaging his sense of safety."

"Jessica, Jessica," she cuts me off. "It's going to be fine. Besides the new case manager has already set it up."

I felt my throat close a little. I was holding back tears. "What do you mean, it's already set up? He's in one of my homes and we are supposed to do the best thing, do what is in his best interest."

"Jessica! Don't you think I have his best interest in mind?"

No, I think. *You are only in it for the extra income a new placement gives you.*

"Listen, it's going to be fine," she says again.

"Alexis, his therapist is not going to agree to this."

"It doesn't matter, his case manager is his legal guardian, and you have to do what she says. She is the one who makes the decisions."

"Alexis..." I start to say, but she cuts me off again, "It's going to be fine," she insists. And then she says, "I'll talk to you later, or perhaps I'll call Elizabeth instead." And then she hangs up.

Years before, Alexis and Elizabeth had worked closely together in our Developmental Foster Home program. They developed a friendship, and then Alexis left the agency. Several of our licensed families left our agency and transferred to Alexis' new agency, Alliance. She poached the families right out from under us. There were some hard feelings, but after a little time Alexis and Elizabeth's friendship resumed.

I was enraged. I was so angry. I balled my fists tightly, stood up, then sat down again. I took a deep breath and began to cry. *Oh Dylan*, I think. *I'm so sorry.* After a few minutes I calmed down, pulled myself together and picked up the phone to call Dylan's foster mom, Christina.

After I finished talking to Christina, who seemed so much calmer than me, I called Dylan's therapist and left a very detailed message. Finally, I called Elizabeth to catch her up to speed. She was as angry as I and couldn't believe Alexis spoke to me that way. While I was on the phone with her and we were getting our frustrations out in a safe space, the phone rang and I click over. It was the therapist. She was not happy about the situation and said we needed to call a meeting. I agreed and said I would come any time she is available. She said to let her handle it.

Three days later on Thursday, we get together at the therapist's office for a formal meeting. The two licensing agencies are present, Alexis and me as the licensing specialists for each family, the therapist is present, Elizabeth has come, as she was Dylan's first licensing specialist and is my supervisor, the DDD Case manager is present (aka the legal guardian), Christina is present, the potential adoptive mother is present and a representative from Dylan's psychiatrist's office is present, who has worked with Dylan, and is familiar with his special needs.

CHAPTER 26

I'M IMPRESSED WE ALL MADE this meeting work, but I have a sick feeling in my stomach. The therapist calls the meeting to order and starts the conversation. What happens over the next 15 minutes brings a range of emotions. All the people who know Dylan are advocating for adoption but with a very slow transition. Of course, we don't oppose a chance at a forever home for him. What we oppose is throwing him to the wolves, I mean, into an unfamiliar setting with people he doesn't know. It took months for him to move through transition with the Maxwells and Browns.

I've mentally divided the people at the table into two sides: those who realistically care about Dylan and his well-being and those who really have no idea who Dylan is. Those who care about Dylan share how he came into care, and the years of painstaking consistency that it has taken to get him to where he is currently. It is also emphasized how important slow transitions are for Dylan to continue his progress and not to cause him to regress. When I hear these arguments I feel pleased and encouraged at the quality of testimony with actual data and examples to back up the positions that put Dylan's needs first.

I was raised to believe that when you present factual data and share it in a way others can understand, they will see the logic and stop pushing for that which is detrimental, nonsense, and dangerous. I experienced this throughout my childhood and into young adulthood. However, the further into adulthood I grew, I realized that logic, experience, and facts weren't held as highly by many individuals I came into contact with.

The potential adoptive mother spoke up, "It doesn't sound like you trust us. We are experienced foster parents. We've been trained. We have worked with children with special needs. We think Dylan will fit in so well with our family. We have so much love to give. And he even looks like us and all our kids."

As she spoke these words my knowing was further confirmed. This wasn't going to work. Dylan wasn't going to be fixed by being loved enough. He was immensely loved by many people, and those people knew what he needed: lots of time and consistency, and a slow transition. Even something as simple as a new student in his classroom at school required a transition process.

The DDD case manager spoke up. "Thank you all for your input, BUT (she raises her voice a bit) I am his legal guardian and he has been in foster care too long. If we don't move now, he may never be adopted. And you said," she says looking at me, "he's adoptable right, Jessica?"

I feel heat spread across my face. "I believe every child is adoptable with the right fit of family."

She smirks at my response, "Right, and I think this will be a good match." She hurries on before I can say anything more. "So, we will move forward with the visit this weekend. If all goes well, I think we can place him within two weeks. Jessica…" she turns to me again. "I understand that you often transport Dylan, but I'm going to ask the adoptive family to pick him up at school on Friday. Christina will be there to let him know it's okay and safe.

At this point, the therapist speaks up. "For the record, this could be a decision that is detrimental to Dylan's health and well-being. I…"

Alexis cuts in and says dismissively, "It's going to be fine. I know Dylan. It's fine."

I'm floored at that statement. Alexis barely interacted with Dylan when he came into care years ago. She doesn't know him. My heart feels like it is a caged animal trying to get out. Others are talking and making necessary arrangements.

I feel compelled to say more, to try and convince the group that we shouldn't move forward this quickly. I can't find an opportunity to butt into the conversation and honestly, I can't find the words. The urge to scream at this group simmers inside me, but all that happens is my eyes water and now I'm focused on not crying.

The following day, Friday, Dylan gets picked up from school by people he's never met, the potential adoptive family. His foster mother, Christina, is there to tell him it's okay.

CHAPTER 27

LATE FRIDAY EVENING DYLAN'S FOSTER mom, Christina, calls me and says that Dylan is home with her. "What? What happened?" I blurt, hearing her chuckle a little on the other end.

"I'm not laughing because it's funny, well, it is a little funny, but the situation isn't funny, sorry. So, apparently after they got home from school Friday, the mom left the kids in the living room playing while she went in the kitchen to go make cookies. Not a minute later she says two kids were crying. One had scratches on his face and the other had a bite on his shoulder."

"Oh no," I say. "Are they okay?"

"Wait," Christina says, "that's not the kicker. She tells Dylan that is not how they behave in their house and he spits at her. She tells him he's in time-out and sits him down in a chair. He gets up and she sits him down again and says, 'If you get up, I'm going to put you to bed with no dinner.' As she bends down to attend to the boy with scratches on his face Dylan picks up a wrench they had laying out and throws it at the mom. It hits her on the head. She said Dylan just laughed at her and said, 'I hate you,' and kept spitting. She called me after that, and I went to get him."

I asked how Dylan was when Christina went to get him. "He seemed fine," she replied, "but he's been very clingy tonight and gagged a couple of times at dinner because he was stuffing his mouth like he used to. He hasn't done that in about a year. We're going to go back to the really small portions again until he gets that under control."

I ask Christina to document any other behaviors she sees over the next few weeks and she says she will.

"This was a bad idea, Jessica," she says.

"I know. The thing is, with some patience it might have been a good idea."

"True," she replies. We hang up the phone.

Three hours later I wake to my phone indicating a message had been received. "Hey, Jessica, it's Christina. You don't have to call me back, I just wanted to let you know that Dylan has forced himself to vomit in the bed, then wet the bed. After we got him cleaned up, he pooped his pants in the bed. But he didn't wake us for that. Instead, he got up and ripped up all the books in his room, sitting in his own mess. If there's anything else, I'll let you know." Her voice sounded tired and a bit resigned.

I lay back down in bed and can't get to sleep until the sun is starting to come up. At 6a.m. the phone rings again and it's the supervisor of Dylan's new case manager. She sounds tired. "Hi, Jessica, I'm sorry to call you so early. I thought I'd get your voicemail." I tell her it's ok and I didn't get much sleep anyway. She tells me the same.

"Listen, I got a very detailed email from the therapist that works with Dylan and I spoke with her on Friday. I'm sorry I was too late to step in. I've heard from Alliance about Dylan's behavior at the potential adoptive home," My voice begins to break in, and she says, "Before you say anything, I understand. I'm familiar with his case and I know what you guys tried to do with the meeting. I know you weren't opposed to the placement but that you counseled caution and wanted a slow transition. I agree with you. I hate to do this but I'm going to pull the case and give it to a different case manager. I don't like to change things so fast, but this was badly handled, and I don't think she will be the best case manager for Dylan. So, if you can give me a couple of weeks, I have a case manager with an opening coming up. She's extremely experienced and she won't put Dylan through this kind of thing. In the meantime, I will be his interim case manager, so just contact me in the next two weeks if you need anything."

I thank her and clarify her contact information.

"One last thing, send your report of this incident to me, please. I think the family he went to might need to be put on a corrective action plan but keep that between us. He needed to be with an adult at all times except during sleep and that was clearly detailed. The wrench ... that's an issue, clearly."

I tell her I'll have the report to her Monday morning so I can add any other behaviors seen during the weekend. I wish her a good weekend and she returns the wish.

It felt like I was waking from a nightmare, but with a real aftermath to deal with. I again lay down, close my eyes and don't wake up until noon. I awake with a jolt and immediately reach for my phone. Zero calls or messages. "Thank God," I mutter to myself.

My husband peeks in the bedroom., "Hungry?" he asks.

"Starving," I reply, and he walks in with burgers.

CHAPTER 28

DYLAN HAD DIFFICULTY SLEEPING THROUGH the night for months after the botched adoption attempt. Right after the incident he would wake up three or four times a night, often getting out of bed and going to other family members' bedrooms. Each time Christina would get up and put him back in bed. It could be likened to having a baby again. But Dylan was no baby. You couldn't just rock him back to sleep. And, when he did get up, he didn't just wander around, and wasn't often quiet.

Slowly, his routine returned to normal. He began sleeping through the nights and seemed to be getting back on track.

One afternoon, about eight months later, I parked in front of the Brown's home. As I entered the grassy front yard, Dylan came running up to me, crashing into my body with his own. He buried his head into my stomach and wrapped his arms around me, squeezing hard. I could feel the wetness of his saliva soak through my shirt and onto my skin underneath. "Awww, Skiska, I love you. Gimme kiss, I kiss you?"

"On the cheek only," I said. "I love you too, Dylan."

"Watch!" he yells as he releases me and runs in the front yard toward where the Brown's dog lay under the tree. The dog had been napping but upon the approach of Dylan the dog got up faster than usual and moved to the side of the house. "Barney, where you going?" He watched as the dog moved away, then directed his attention to the tree. It was a tree made for climbing and the family's kids had all climbed on it over the years. Now it was Dylan's turn. He said loudly, "Look, look at me!" He reached his arms up to a low, fat branch and sort of hugged it. He raised one leg up to the lowest spot where the branch grew from the trunk. His foot slipped off and his hands gave up as he fell back onto the ground. "Hep me! Hep, hep me, I need hep!"

He looked to me and Christina who had been sitting on a bench on the front porch. I started to move forward and Christina replied, "No, you can do it on your own, remember? And if you can't do it, then you'll just have to practice."

I stopped moving forward. I wouldn't interfere with a foster parent's or parent's instruction unless it was detrimental or dangerous to the child. Dylan tried again as Christina told me he had been able to get up a couple of times by holding his legs up and arms on the branch, sort of like an underside hug. He'd done it the day before, in fact, Christina shared.

Before doing it on his own two of the older foster brothers had been helping him more, but they stopped after he bit them both. Christina figured the practice on his own was a good strength builder. I agreed. I asked her about the biting and why she hadn't told me. She said they weren't serious enough. The first was to the younger son, who was about three years older than Dylan. As he was helping Dylan grasp onto a branch, he moved Dylan's hand to a better position. As he did this, Dylan leaned his head down to the boy's hand. When he felt the warm wetness of Dylan's mouth and saliva, and next the hard teeth pressing against the skin on the back of his hand, he jerked his hand back, wiped it on his pants and called for his mom. The very faint indentation of a row of teeth was visible, but quickly disappeared. Dylan, whose feet hadn't left the ground, turned toward his foster brother and started spitting at him. Christina was already at the door, as she had been keeping an eye on them through a window. She said that she had called to Dylan and he came running to her, saliva running down his chin.

The second sort of bite occurred with the next older Brown son, who was five years older than Dylan. He had put Dylan on this back, piggyback style, to help him get on the tree. As he was instructing Dylan where to place his hands and feet,

Dylan bent his head down and bit the boy's shoulder through his sweatshirt. The bite was really just to the clothing. It took place the day after the first bite to the younger brother.

Sitting on the bench beside Christina, she turns to me and says, "I know what you were saying when Dylan first came to us. That sometimes he would act out of frustration at his lack of his own abilities. But also, he might act out when he felt unsafe or unsure. Sometimes I see him act out at times when he seems fine. When I can't see a clear frustration or fear, or even overexcitement. He doesn't even act out always when he knows I'm watching. I'm having a hard time anticipating him and when he might act out."

I asked what the most obvious behaviors were that she was now seeing. Mostly hitting, kicking, scratching, and spitting. Next would be biting and lastly urinating and fecal smearing.

"Fecal smearing?" I asked. "He hasn't done that for a very long time. When did this happen?"

"Two weeks ago. He got mad because I took his stuffed dog away," she tells me. The stuffed dog was such a comfort to him, like a security blanket. I listened as she described what happened.

"After dinner our whole family was watching TV. Dylan kept talking and I asked him to stop because we were all watching the show. He kept at it, so I sent him to his room. Usually, he will go and either play or empty his drawers, nothing too destructive anymore. Well, this time he pulled the sheets off his bed and his brother's bed and began ripping up papers and posters. He was only in there for about three minutes. I hadn't heard anything. When I went in and saw what he had done I was pretty angry. He was sitting on the floor hitting his stuffed dog and then hugging it, then biting it and hugging it. I told him he needed to calm down or I was going to take the dog away. He yelled at me, 'I hate you' and started spitting at me. I took the dog and told him it was time for bed.

"He became enraged. His face was so red, and he was screaming at me for his dog. I said not until he calmed down.

I told him to go to the bathroom and brush his teeth for bed. He went there and after a minute I heard him laughing and making sort of pounding sounds on the wall. When I opened the door, it was everywhere. The toilet, the walls, the rug, the sink, the door, the shower curtain. I've never seen anything like it. I almost threw up at the smell. He was just sitting on the floor rubbing his hands on the rug. He looked up at me and said, 'Hi mom, you hep me?'"

Christina was gazing into the yard to where Dylan was still attempting to climb the tree, but not really focusing on him.

"Christina…." I began.

"You don't have to say it, Jessica. He's been here over two years and I've never seen him like this." I only wanted to offer her support at this point. "Did you talk with the therapist about it this week?"

"On the phone. Our appointment was cancelled because she was sick. She reminded me that he doesn't comprehend the same way other kids do. The rules are different for him and we have to go so slow. I thought we were making so much progress." Christina had just said what had been said to her several times by me and Dylan's therapists. *She's finally getting it,* I thought.

Her shoulders dropped and she looked tired and defeated. She started again. "I know. I know Dylan's different. But I know he can get it, he can learn."

"Yes," I stop her. "He can learn. He has been learning. All the progress he's made with you guys isn't gone."

"I feel like it is gone," she said. "I feel like we're starting over. Like he's trying to teach me a lesson."

"In a way you may be starting over," I say. She looks at me. "What I mean is that you may have to revert back to the training you used nearly a year ago. I'd be willing to bet that he catches on faster, and you get back to where you were in a month or two."

She throws her hands up. "A month or two? Why did he move backwards? Why?"

"It makes sense, actually. There have been big changes in his world. His therapy has moved into a new phase and he's only had this therapist for about six months. That's one thing." I hold my thumb up. "Dr. Springer changed his meds only three months ago. That's two." I hold my forefinger against my thumb. "He has a new DDD case manager. That's three."

Christina breaks in. "He hasn't even met the new worker."

"I know," I say, "but you and I have talked about it while Dylan has been nearby. And the other case manager said good-bye to Dylan, he gets what that means on some level. You just had spring break and went camping with the family and Dylan stayed with the respite caregiver. That's four. That happened only four weeks ago. Even though the caregiver is experienced, it's not the same as being home."

Christina nods her head and focuses her eyes on Dylan again. "We'll keep plugging away."

CHAPTER 29

MONTHS LATER, CHRISTINA CALLED ME and said that their normal respite provider was not going to be available as much. Whether that meant she was really unavailable or just unavailable for Dylan, I didn't know. What we did know is that Dylan needed a new respite provider, they needed to be extremely well-trained and patient, and a bonus if they had the soul of a saint. The Browns used a respite provider two to three times each month. Sometimes it was for a few hours and other times it was overnight.

I told her that I would start looking and inquiring with other agencies for respite providers who might meet our needs. She said she would inquire with other foster families, too. Soon, someone was found. A single woman who was licensed as a foster-care provider was open to providing respite care. She had one foster child, a male teen who had been with her for some time.

Lucinda was kind and seemed to have the qualifications we were looking for. When I met her, I noticed how quiet she was, and I wondered at her abilities but was willing to give almost anyone a try who met our criteria for Dylan. Christina arranged for a couple of meet-and-greets. The first visit was at the Brown's home and one at Lucinda's home. Christina said Dylan seemed to take to Lucinda right away and set up a respite day. It was going to be for several hours while the Browns attended an award banquet for one of their children at school.

The day of the banquet I picked up Dylan from school and drove him to Lucinda's house. Dylan asked, "We going to

McDonalds?" I replied, "Today, I'm taking you to Lucinda's house."

"No," Dylan said, "I want Kistina." I reminded him that Christina and the family were at his foster brother's school, but that they would come pick him up after dinner. "Sinda?" Dylan pronounced her name.

"Yes, Lucinda." He didn't seem agitated. I asked how school was that day.

Dylan replied, "I like school." Then he named a few children in his class.

Over the past year, Dylan's behavior during car rides had drastically changed. He mostly just asked questions over and over. "What that say?" "Why?" "Where we going?" It was enjoyable. When we got to Lucinda's home, I said, "We're here."

"We here?" Dylan asked.

"Yep. Can you get unbuckled?"

"I do it," he replied, fumbling with the buckle and releasing himself.

He dragged his backpack with one hand and held my hand with the other as we walked up to the door. I reached out to push the doorbell and Dylan said, "I do it!" pushing the doorbell several times.

"Dylan, let's take a break. Lucinda only needs the button to be pushed once, maybe twice." He was still pushing the doorbell and I covered his hand with mine as the door opened.

"Hi," said Lucinda.

"Sindaaa..." Dylan said and stepped into give her a hug, then handed her his backpack. "Hi, Lucinda," I said. She smiled at me and held the backpack out to Dylan, telling him to put it on the couch and they would take a look inside.

I stayed for several minutes and before leaving checked to make sure she had all the necessary numbers and asked if there was anything she needed or had questions about. She shook her head and said, "No, I don't think so."

"Please call me or Christina if you need anything," I said.

"Okay," she replied.

"Bye, Dylan," I called, and he ran to the door, squeezing me with a hug. "Bye, Skiska."

I walked to my car feeling apprehensive. "That was too easy," I said to myself. I pulled out of the driveway and headed back to the office. I thought I'd stay on this side of town just in case something happened, but, nothing did. At 7 p.m. I headed home for the weekend.

CHAPTER 30

THE FOLLOWING WEEK I MET with Christina for our monthly monitoring visit. We went over hers and her husband's need for CPR and First Aid renewal, and other licensing updates. The conversation continued on to Dylan. I had made the appointment to see her during school hours so we could talk about Dylan without him around.

Christina said the weekend was great. She also said that Dylan talked about Lucinda several times, and she planned to use her again soon. I expressed how pleased I was to hear this.

"Jessica, I think Lucinda might be a candidate for a forever home for Dylan," she said.

"What?" I wasn't comprehending.

Christina continued, "She's had the other boy for several years and I think he's aging out soon. When that happens she's thinking of changing her license to a developmental home license instead."

"Wow, good for her, but what am I missing here? Things have calmed down a lot with Dylan and you all seem to be getting into a groove now."

Christina begins, "You know that Eric (Christina's husband) has been traveling to Texas like every other month for his job? Well, he told me the company wants to move him to Texas permanently when the guy over there retires. It won't be for about six more months."

"Oh, my gosh, that's exciting news. Have you considered adopting Dylan?" I ask, hopefully.

"Briefly, but you know when we got into foster care it was more for kids who needed short-term placements. We never thought we'd have a child for this long, not to mention someone of Dylan's needs. We love him, but no. We never planned to adopt, and we still feel the same way."

"Okay," I said, my mind starting to race.

Christina cut into my thoughts. "Look, this isn't happening right now. We have time, and I think it is a good thing to expand Dylan's circle. Especially now that he has been doing so well and seems to be maturing some."

Her words made so much sense and she was right. Dylan's circle did need to expand. He would need that to happen over and over again to build his network. The goal was to help him become as self-sufficient as possible, to be able to integrate into society as independently as he could. Christina was right.

My mind flipped back to the fiasco, two years before, we had endured alongside Dylan, how horribly it had gone. Now, where we were collectively, Dylan's team and Dylan; the progress was remarkable. The incidents of his behaviors were down to only a few times a month and the severity could be characterized as "difficult but manageable". Transitions were still a trigger for him (a change in teachers, a change in routine) but the impact was less and the time it took for him to move through the stages was much shorter.

I left the home visit with some apprehension at the edges of my mind and heart. When I got back to the office, I sent an email out to schedule the next Child Family Team meeting, then began listing what needed to happen to make this upcoming transition as smooth as possible for Dylan.

CHAPTER 31

DYLAN'S SMILE TOOK OVER HIS whole face. He smiled so much, and his blue eyes sparkled like a swimming pool in the sun. He had grown from a child, very small for his age, to a middle-school kid slightly shorter than his peers. His balance was more stable. The past three years with the Browns seemed to me just what he had needed. He had been challenged, nurtured, and allowed to grow. Jane Maxwell had been right three years ago. They had taken him as far as they were meant to, and the Browns had taken the baton and run with it, getting Dylan closer and closer to a finish line. What that finish line is, I don't know. Is it permanence, a forever home and family? Is it graduation from high school, or beyond? Is the finish line Dylan living alone, able to care for himself, holding a job? Is it more than that? The sky is the limit, isn't it? Because he's diagnosed with a developmental disability, does that mean there is a cap on how far he can go? I never felt comfortable with the idea of a cap on one's journey. Is there really a finish line in life?

Some might suggest there is. Death. Others might suggest it occurs before death, when a person plateaus in life. Who determines what that plateau is? Isn't the very act of living to the next day, and the next day, and the next day, proof that progress continues? The next day that you have lived to has never existed before. It is brand new for everyone. It may feel the same to many people, but that's perception.

Dylan has no finish line as far as I am concerned.

The Browns did move to Texas, and Dylan was transitioned to Lucinda's care. The transition took place long before the Browns moved. This was ideal, because Christina then filled the role of a respite provider for Lucinda. The family even brought Dylan to their home occasionally to spend time together. It was the best possible transition scenario that could have happened with the circumstances given.

When Dylan transitioned to Lucinda, he transitioned out of my agency's care and responsibility. Lucinda was licensed through another agency. She shared her desire to be a forever home for Dylan, and would consider adoption, but needed time to take things slow and wanted to make sure it was in both their best interests. She tried to explain the special connection she had felt the first time she met Dylan but felt she couldn't quite find the words to capture it.

I felt some relief when he transitioned to Lucinda, and then I felt guilt at feeling the relief. And then I felt a deep sadness outlined with hope and love. He was leaving our larger family at the agency. We had known him since he was just four years old. He was now almost a teenager.

"Skiska…" I still hear his pronunciation of my name, floating in my head every once in a while. When it comes to me, I remember his smile, his golden hair in the sun, his eyes sparkling and his crushing hugs with a cool spot of saliva on my torso. When I'm feeling frustrated by a situation with no way out but to trudge on, I sometimes remember the day in the car, the saliva flying from the backseat to splash on my cheek and coating my hair, and I feel empowered to keep on going.

Dylan has.

ACKNOWLEDGMENTS

FOR MORE THAN A FEW years now, I've been part of a small group of authors offering support, mentorship, and encouragement. Linda Curry and David McArthur, thank you for the guidance and most of all for consistently "being there" without expectation. I have reached this point in large part to both of you.

To my family and friends who have offered encouragement, asked questions, provided inspiration, and shared their thoughts, thank you. I am deeply grateful. Your continued interest provided much needed momentum.

For my husband, Kevin, who was very much part of my journey while working with "Dylan", as well as the journey to complete this book. Without you we would not be holding this book in our hands.

ABOUT THE AUTHOR

GROWING UP IN SEVERAL STATES in the U.S., Jessica's own childhood has provided valuable experiences and perspectives that have allowed her to connect with others from a variety of backgrounds. She holds degrees in Early Childhood Education and Sociology in addition to multiple certifications to support the health and development of families and children.

As an artist and nature lover, Jessica often engages with children and adults through creating something new or by getting outside and recognizes the therapeutic benefits that art and nature can provide for others as well as herself.

Jessica lives with her husband in Arizona and enjoys hiking, gardening, travel, and testing new recipes on family and friends.